AMERICAN COUNTRY STORES

by Bruce Roberts and Ray Jones

———

STEEL SHIPS AND IRON MEN:
*A Tribute to World War II Fighting Ships and
the Men Who Served on Them*

NORTHERN LIGHTHOUSES:
New Brunswick to the Jersey Shore

SOUTHERN LIGHTHOUSES:
From Chesapeake Bay to the Gulf of Mexico

AMERICAN
COUNTRY STORES

photographs by Bruce Roberts

text by Ray Jones

The
Globe
Pequot
Press

CHESTER, CONNECTICUT

Photo credits: pp. 4, 24—Gale Trussell-TVA-VRC;
p. 20—Colonial Williamsburg Foundation, Williamsburg, Va.;
p. 35—Vermont Division for Historical Preservation;
pp. 77–78—Art Meripol; pp. 96–97, 98—U.S. Department of Interior,
National Park Service, Hubbell Trading Post NHS, photo numbers
HUTR-RP-54 & HUTR-RP-14; pp. 99, 100—Kelly Weaver;
p. 101—Jeff Paslay; pp. 102–3—Kevin Cannon

Library of Congress Cataloging-in-Publication Data

Roberts, Bruce. 1930-
        American country stores/photographs by
Bruce Roberts; text by Ray Jones.—1st ed.
                p.   cm.
        Includes appendix.
        ISBN 0-87106-228-3
        1. General stores—United States—History. 2. Retail
trade—United States—History. I. Jones, Ray, 1948-
II. Title.
HF5429.3.R58   1991
381'.1'0973—dc20   91-12279
                                                        CIP
                                                        AC

Front cover: the Old Sautee Store, Sautee, Georgia
Book design, Nancy Freeborn
Cover Design, Regine de Toledo
Printed and bound in Hong Kong by Everbest Printing Co. Ltd.
First Edition/First Printing

To Fran

CONTENTS

This book is dedicated to the preservation of a rich American tradition: the country store. Now only a memory, the delightful Yancy County Country Store, shown above, served generations in Burnsville, North Carolina, until it was gutted by fire in 1985. While unhappy accidents, hard economic realities, and the ravages of time have destroyed more than a few, many of the nation's finest old stores have survived, as you'll see on the pages that follow.

FOREWORD

by Tom Bodett

It was Mark Twain who said that the one thing we all have in common is a childhood. But, as this volume shows, it's not the only thing. Fact is, memories of country stores, like the smell of gas dripped on hot gravel and the taste of watermelon on a summer's night, are also fixed permanently in the American mind. Now Bruce Roberts and Ray Jones awaken those memories with these images of country stores.

Even those among us who can't honestly claim to have visited a country store can somehow invent the experience and make it our own. Bring up the subject at any kitchen table gathering and see how clearly this rings true. These rural outposts or their city cousins, the Mom-and-Pop stores, seem to have been the scene of everybody's first brush with the principles of business and exchange. Remember trying to buy a half-cent jawbreaker with a whole penny? Or figuring out whether two-cents worth of rock candy at ten cents per pound would be enough for the whole gang? Or working a red wagon down the shoulder of the road, combing the ditches for returnable bottles? At the end of the road stood the store that would redeem your labors for a few dimes. The terror of balancing on the bottle crates next to the old pop machine on the porch was offset by the knowledge that one solid tug at just the right moment would release the ice-cold prize. Anything less and the machine would eat your dimes and send you hat-in-hand to the proprietor for an embarrassing refund and a welcome second chance.

Family road trips to Grandma's or Aunt Gert's were often highlighted by stops at such curious little emporiums. Mom wouldn't trust the rest room, and she'd urge everyone to hold out for the Texaco station at the interchange. But who could wait?

On your way out the screened door, Popsicles in hand, you'd see friendly men in familiar chairs who always managed to say something to raise a blush and to suggest that you had been a welcome distraction. The Popsicles never made it as far as the Texaco station.

It's reassuring to see that these simpler times have not gone the way of twenty-cent gas and half-cent jawbreakers. Turn the pages of this book and you'll see that they haven't gone away at all.

INTRODUCTION
A Penny's Worth of Licorice

The screen door of the old country store groaned as it closed behind two small boys, one of them pinching a penny hard between his thumb and forefinger. Tow-headed and freckle-faced, the boys approached the counter, their bare feet shuffling over the wooden floor. Standing at the register, an aproned keeper stood scowling at them, his hands on his hips.

"How much is your licorice?" asked the boy with the penny. He was barely tall enough to peer over the edge of the counter.

The keeper almost succeeded in hiding his smile behind a thick mustache. "Two strings for a penny," he said.

John Steinbeck put a scene similar to this one into his classic Depression-era novel, *The Grapes of Wrath*, but he was not the first to tell the story. In one version or another this simple anecdote and thousands of others like it have been told over and over. Stories that take us up to the counter of a country store are timeless; most of them might have been told a century, even two centuries, ago as easily as today. Perhaps that is because the country store is such an enduring institution. Like baseball and the Thanksgiving turkey, it is part of that vague notion each of us clings to of what it is to be American.

For every child who ever pushed through the door of a country store, there is an adult with rich, sensual memories of the experience: the aromas of home-baked bread, freshly ground coffee, spices, and aging wood; the bright colors of cans

"My customers are my friends," said old-time North Carolina shopkeeper Joe Young (left). Such neighborly attitudes still welcome shoppers to rural businesses like Virginia's Sugar Tree Country Store (right).

Warm wood and cool refreshment beckon customers at Betty's Country Store in the north Georgia mountains.

and cartons lining shelves that often reached all the way to the ceiling; the sweetness of candy bars, bubble gum, and homemade fudge; the buttery flavor of packaged crackers, cashews, and popcorn; the refreshing chill of soft drinks lifted from deep inside a frosty cooler; or the warmth thrown out like a wooly blanket from a wood-burning stove. There is plenty of human warmth to remember as well: old men who gathered around stoves to whittle, chew tobacco, and tell stories; crusty clerks who asked a modest price for a hunk of cheese sliced from a large wheel but charged nothing at all for the latest gossip or a piece of advice; and keepers who, if they liked, could sell anything at all for a penny.

You may think the old-fashioned country store with its neighborly keeper, checkerboard, and penny candy is *only* a memory. Happily, such is not the case. Many fine old stores have survived the rush of America's rural population to cities and supermarkets. Some continue to flourish under the guidance of the same families who have operated them for generations. Other stores that long ago lost their battle with what is often called "progress" have recently had the boards pulled off their windows; a new, energetic breed of owners—often young, idealistic husband-and-wife teams—have dusted them out, rekindled their stoves, and restocked their ceiling-high shelves with merchandise.

Country stores often remain surprisingly true to their origins. The oldest and most authentic of them might be described as living history museums of nineteenth- or early twentieth-century America. Stopping by one of these vintage stores for a bag of salty peanuts and a cold soft drink can be both entertaining and educational. Most still have plenty of old-time country experiences to offer. For instance, you can still buy crackers from a barrel at the Vermont Country Store in Weston, eat cheddar cheese so sharp it will "bite your tongue" at the Petersham (Massachusetts) Store, listen as banjo wizards stomp their feet at the Todd (North Carolina) General Store, or warm your paws beside a potbellied stove at the Mast General Store in nearby Valle Crucis. You can sit a spell on the loafing stools at the Hevener Store in High-

town, Virginia, pick out a handwoven wool horse blanket at the Hubbell Trading Post on the Navaho Reservation in Arizona, or buy a bottle of pickled okra at the Pomona (Illinois) General Store and have your purchase totaled on a polished brass cash register that can handle only $9.99 worth of merchandise at a time.

These are only a few of the delights waiting alongside back roads from the Blue Ridge Mountains of Virginia to the gold-rush country of California. From New England to Texas, Florida to Oregon, every state in every region has country stores worth a visit. But the best of them are rarely located near the exits of four-lane interstates. To reach them, you must travel roads with

A hot pot-bellied stove warms the heart of the Hevener Store, west of the Virginia Blue Ridge.

faded center lines and pockmarked stop signs at railroad crossings. This book is written in hopes of encouraging you to brave those roads and make your own discoveries. But for now, we invite you to kick back with a handful of crackers and a nibble of cheese—or maybe a twist of chewy licorice—and join us as we go home to America's country stores.

Weathered posters (above) displayed at Georgia's Old Sautee Store recall earlier times.

The "Old Days" live on for these country gentlemen (right), who have "settled in for a spell to chew the fat" on the porch of a store near Knoxville, Tennessee.

On the Way Home . . .

WHERE GREAT-GRANDFATHER SHOPPED

Through History's Screen Door

When customers open the door of **Peltier's Market** in Vermont's tiny village of Dorset, it creaks and groans convincingly, as if to remind them that countless others have pushed through it before them. Indeed, the market has stood beside Dorset's village common long enough to attract a great many shoppers. The wooden sign hanging above the awnings out front reads 1816, and that's not the street number. This store has been selling flour, sugar, beans, nails, buckets, boots, and an occasional luxury item since about the time James Monroe was elected president—more than 175 years ago.

With its crisp, white clapboard walls, pitched roof, dark green shutters, and bright canvas awnings, Peltier's seems too old and too pretty to be a business. It's hard not to think of it as some sort of museum. But the air in its aisles carries no musty museum smells. Instead, it hints of just-baked bread, freshly ground coffee, and sometimes even Texas-style chili. Overhead, fluorescent light glows cool and white. The shelving and furnishings are veterans but do not look as if they were purchased at an antique shop or estate sale; most have never had another home.

Peltier's makes no attempt to present itself as anything more than what it is—a small-town market. People come here to buy hamburger buns, salad dressing, canned tomatoes, fresh celery, self-rising flour, measuring cups, whisk brooms, and birthday candles—whatever they might need to put dinner on the table or to make their houses and lives a little more livable. Some of these items could be had cheaper and in greater variety at stores in Manchester, a much larger town only about fifteen miles away. But Peltier's customers believe their store offers extras that no supermarket could ever hope to match. For one thing, storekeeper Jay Hathaway knows

A rainbow of candies, fresh bakery goods, tins of maple syrup, and owner Jay Hathaway welcome customers to the counter at Peltier's Market.

Jellybeans and other Peltier's delights complete a summer's day for these Dorset youngsters.

their names and is also likely to know when someone in their family is ill, when a child has lost a tooth, or when company is coming. That's because his customers are also his neighbors.

To many customers the store itself is a neighbor, a very old and highly regarded one. A sizable number of Dorset folks have family roots in this village that reach back for generations. For them, a daily stop at Peltier's is a time-honored tradition. The old clapboard market affords them a pleasure and comfort available to very few shoppers anywhere nowadays: that of buying eggs and milk in the same store where their great-grandparents also bought eggs and milk. "It's like stepping into a photograph on the back page of a family album," says one Peltier's regular.

A Peddler's Wagon without Wheels

Few early communities were as remote as Dorset, which stood on the west side of Vermont's spine of rugged mountains. As was the case in rural settlements throughout America, however, the first store appeared just as soon as the village had enough people to support one. In Dorset that happened during the late 1700s, when marble was discovered in the nearby mountains and a small quarrying operation began to attract workers. The stonecutters bought food and other necessities at one of two Dorset houses, hastily converted for use as general stores.

The store known today as Peltier's Market did not appear until 1816. The building is thought to have been moved from East Rupert, about five miles to the west, where it had also served as a store. Its first Dorset owners were Norman Blackmer and his partner, Harvey Holley. They bought bulk foods and dry goods from wholesale houses in Boston and other cities and had them shipped to Dorset by wagon. The merchandise was then profitably resold a little at a time to village residents and nearby farmers. No doubt, Blackmer and Holley did most of the work at the store themselves: keeping the books, stocking the shelves, sweeping the floors, and, of course, waiting on customers personally.

In addition to Blackmer and Holley, at least thirteen owners or ownership groups have run the store. From 1833 to 1839, and again from 1851 to 1858, it was operated by a cooperative called the Dorset Union, which sold memberships to citizens for $10 each. Members could buy groceries and other merchandise at six percent above cost, and they received a small annual return on their investment. For most of its one-and-three-quarter centuries, however, the store has been run by owner/operators like Blackmer and Holley. Today's owners, Jay Hathaway and his wife, Terri, fall into the latter tradition.

Nowadays, the store's merchandise is delivered by trucks instead of wagons. Most food items are prepackaged and do not need to be doled out to customers from barrels, boxes, and bins as in the days of Blackmer and Holley. But otherwise, the Hathaways continue to run their store in much the same way that it and most other country stores have always been run. "We've tried to keep things the way they were," says Jay Hathaway, who bought the store in 1977. "Peltier's belongs to the town and to its own past as much as it does to us."

The Hathaways, like many old-time storekeeping families before them, actually live in their store. Sections of the second and third floors have been converted into a spacious apartment complete with a gourmet kitchen and wide, airy deck. Terri Hathaway has an office in the building, where she keeps the store's books up-to-date. Her office furniture is made from old wire display racks. The Hathaway children often work at the store and, like their parents, know most of the store's customers on a first-name basis. An interior designer, Mr. Hathaway maintains a nicely appointed office in an upstairs room. But, like Blackmer and Holley, he also stocks shelves, waits on customers, and, yes, often sweeps the floors at day's end.

When customers got wheels, store owners were quick to cash in with gas pumps such as this antique at the Florence Cilley Store in Plymouth, Vermont. Ironically, the advent of the automobile spelled doom for many country stores by giving rural folks access to cities and supermarkets.

A Civil War Storekeeper

In a back room at Peltier's is a picture of firm-featured Gilbert Sykes, who owned and operated the store from 1858 to 1913. When Sykes took over the business, just a few years before the Civil War, Dorset was a robust community with a gristmill, wagon shop, marble quarry, and dairy association capable of producing 125,000 pounds of cheese annually. It had a population of 2,200, nearly a third more people than live in the town today. Account books and shipping bills still on file at the store indicate that Mr. Sykes was able to sell a great variety of merchandise, including boots, shoes, pants, shirts, hardware, crockery, glassware, iron tools, and plows, in addition to medicines and groceries.

Because much of the store's business was done on credit, customers' names and purchases were often written down. For instance, various entries for 1859 show that, on January 24, Steven Jones took pork and tobacco worth 93 cents; on January 25, John Hayes bought a knife for 37 cents; on June 9, J. R. Wilkins charged a pair of boots for $2.54; on August 4, Frank Jones bought a more expensive pair of boots for $2.87; on December 16, Christopher Jones bought five pounds of apples for 40 cents; on December 18, John Moon bought a shirt for 75 cents; on December 21, Christopher Jones bought a box of snuff for 13 cents, and he returned on Christmas Eve to buy a pipe for 38 cents. All of these charged items were eventually paid for in full.

Ledger entries and bills from 1859 indicate that Mr. Sykes's business remained brisk at that time in spite of a nationwide financial crisis. On his cash books for 1859, a year of severe economic recession, Sykes registered $25 in receipts for

December 21, and $34.59 for December 22. The store was closed on Sunday, December 23, but open on Christmas Eve and Christmas Day, when Sykes took in a total of $51.50, a respectable volume of business for a small, mid-1800s country store.

The store's modest, though steady, trade enabled Sykes to keep his shelves well stocked. To do so, he dealt with manufacturers and wholesalers in several northeastern cities. Yellowed order forms and invoices record his purchases. For instance, on May 7, 1859, Sykes ordered five dozen bottles of "gargling oil" for $16.83 from the Merchants Gargling Oil Company of Lockport, New York. On December 13, 1859, he bought four dozen diaries and "writing books" for $6.12 from the G. A. Tuttle Company in Rutland, Vermont. Boston's Nathaniel Lamson & Company charged Sykes $18.64 for four dozen milled files, shipped on October 1, 1860.

Even the gathering storm clouds of civil war did little to dampen business at the Dorset store. At the height of the crucial fall political campaign of 1860, Sykes placed a hefty order with the wholesale grocery firm of Squires, Sherry, and Galusha in Troy, New York. The order included sugar, rice, raisins, peanuts, Brazil nuts, cord, rope, and about a dozen other commodities that Sykes knew he could sell quickly. He paid $62.95 for the shipment, receiving it on October 30, 1860, only a few days before Abraham Lincoln was elected president of the United States. By December 28, 1860, when the J. M. Warren Company, another Troy firm, sent Mr. Sykes six shovels and a dozen axes, the Union had already begun to unravel. War broke out a few months later, and many of the able-bodied men of Dorset and similar small communities all over New England donned blue uniforms and marched southward. No doubt, Mr. Sykes sold buttons, scarves, boots, and shoes to some of the men who would fight and die for the Union.

The Civil War deprived Mr. Sykes of a number of customers—some of them permanently—but it did not fatally wound his business. It remained prosperous and, as many country stores

They began to disappear about the middle of this century, but country stores are enjoying a revival. Customers find them more personal and relaxing than city markets. The porch rocker and geraniums at the Cilley Store in Vermont make the point perfectly.

have done for their owners, made Mr. Sykes a prominent figure in his community. In fact, he became well known throughout western Vermont and eventually served the region as state senator. Sykes's political success, however, did not cause him to abandon or neglect his primary occupation—that of storekeeper. He ran his store for a total of sixty-five years, right up until 1913, when he retired at age seventy-nine.

Only one other Dorset storekeeper has approached Mr. Sykes's record for longevity. Perry Peltier, whose father bought the store from Sykes in 1913, worked at or owned the store for nearly sixty years before he, in turn, sold it to the Hathaways in 1977. Mr. Peltier is well remembered. Older Dorset townsfolk still wince at the thought of his cigar ashes, which sometimes peppered his otherwise high-quality ground beef. It is said that he ripped his bibbed aprons up the middle so that he could pull them on without taking his cigar out of his mouth. The story is still told of a customer who approached Mr. Peltier one day with a complaint. "Perry," said the dissatisfied customer, "the cream I bought yesterday was sour."

"Don't feel bad," replied the keeper. "So was mine."

Drink Coca-Cola? If this pretty lady says so, why not? Antique advertisements such as this one still catch the customer's eye in some country stores.

A COUNTRY-STORE
SAMPLER

Country Store on a Horse's Back

The earliest European settlers on North America's eastern shores traded directly with sea captains who arrived sporadically with supplies brought from across the Atlantic. As active ports grew into towns and then cities such as Boston, Baltimore, and Charleston, merchants opened retail stores where they sold imported goods and a few locally produced items. But patrons could regularly visit these stores only if they lived nearby and had access to money—that rarest of commodities in the American colonies.

Settlers marching steadily to the West soon cut themselves off from the coast and thus from the commerce carried on there by sea traders and seaport shopkeepers. Most of these pioneers were subsistence farmers, and even if there had been a store close by, they would have had no money to spend in it. They did have something of value, however: fur pelts taken in great numbers from dense forests and mountains that teemed with game. Enterprising peddlers saw a tempting opportunity in this trade gap between the cities on the coast and isolated inland farm communities. Loading knapsacks or saddlebags with needles, pins, buttons, knives, and other small items of relatively little value on the coast, they set off for the interior. On foot or horseback, they plodded over faint, lightly traveled trails from one remote outpost to the next. The farther inland they got, the more valuable their wares became.

When approaching a farm or settlement, the peddlers whistled, sang, or blew horns to attract customers and, no doubt, to avoid being mistaken for Indian raiders and shot. Having announced themselves, they were nearly always welcome, for they brought spices, tea, and other reminders of civilization. The peddlers, however, did not relinquish their little treasures easily. Since they had no competitors, they could drive a hard bargain indeed. A woman's whalebone comb or a couple of ordinary spoons might fetch a fancy price in otter or beaver pelts. When the peddlers had bartered for as many fur pelts as they or their horses could carry, they turned back toward the ports in the East. There the pelts were sold, usually for many times the value of the modest goods that had been traded for them.

Gradually, the narrow, backwoods tracks widened into roads, and as travel conditions improved, peddlers gave up their knapsacks and saddlebags in favor of wagons. Now they could carry kettles, saws, hammers, nails, firearms, black powder, and even a few luxuries such as china, cloth, and clocks. Loaded down with tea, tobacco, and a clanking abundance of pots, pans, utensils, and other general merchandise, their wagons rumbled and rattled from farm to farm, village to village.

Increasingly, peddlers found they could sell their wares for money instead of bartering them for pelts and other goods. With silver in their pockets and no furs to freight back to the port cities in the East, the wandering merchants soon grew weary of the road. Like the pioneer farmers before them, they began to yearn for a piece of ground to call their own. Some of them pulled out adzes, planes, and hammers—perhaps from their own sales stocks—and set to work on buildings to house their merchandise. In promising villages, beside gristmills, or at crossroads, they built one-room structures or, more often, houses with one or more rooms set aside for business. These were the first true country stores.

The earliest country stores offered bulk foods and supplies as well as simple manufactured goods, many of them made locally. Reproductions of authentic 1830s-era wares, these brooms and wooden farm tools can be seen at Old Sturbridge Village in Massachusetts.

The Same Location since 1740

More history has been seen through the display windows of the **Prentis Store** in Williamsburg, Virginia, than through most windows at the White House. George Washington and Thomas Jefferson often walked past the store's windows and may occasionally have been tempted by something they saw there to step inside and spend a little money—pounds sterling before the Revolution and Continental dollars afterwards. During the Revolutionary War, General Cornwallis's "Death or Glory" dragoons charged in front of the windows, and later, generals Washington and Lafayette brought their armies by on the way to Yorktown. During the Civil War, a contingent of Union cavalry galloped past, led by the flamboyant George Armstrong Custer, who some years later would keep an appointment with the Sioux at the Little Bighorn in Montana.

Today's Prentis Store visitors may or may not be destined to make history, but they *are* likely to catch a glimpse of it. More than 250 years old, the exterior of the building has been restored to its original appearance by the Colonial Williamsburg Foundation. The store's shelves are lined with salt-glazed pottery and many other products identical to or very like those that prosperous Virginians bought more than two centuries ago. And it's all for sale. The store still functions as a retail business, much as it did before the American Revolution.

Among the oldest retail outlets in America, the store owes its existence in no small measure to the efforts of William Prentis, an English orphan who in 1714, at age fifteen, signed on as a clerk with a prominent Williamsburg merchant. Mr. Prentis eventually became manager and part owner of the business. It was under his guidance that, in 1740, a new brick store was built facing Williamsburg's Duke of Gloucester Street. Constructed for about 200 pounds sterling, a large sum at the time, the building resembled in some of its details the homes of wealthy colonials. The Prentis Store maintained a brisk trade in tea, tobacco, cloth, pottery, and a host of other "civilized" items.

Restored to its 1740s appearance, the Prentis Store in Colonial Williamsburg sells wares typical of that time.

The store remained in the Prentis family for several decades after America won its independence from the British, finally passing to new owners in 1809, the same year that Thomas Jefferson handed the presidency over to James Madison. In time it would serve as an apothecary and be put to many other commercial uses. During the 1920s it was used as a service station and auto parts store, and signs advertising oil and tires were painted on its old brick walls. Luckily, for those of us who love country stores, it has now been restored to serve its original purpose.

*Inside and out, the **Asa Knight Store** looks much as it did 150 years ago when Asa Knight ran it. Mr. Knight prospered as a storekeeper until he made the mistake of expanding his operation just as the storm of a nationwide financial panic was about to break. Mr. Knight died in 1851, but his son managed to keep the store open until 1863. During the present century, the store was moved from its original location in Dummerston, Vermont, to Old Sturbridge Village in Massachusetts, a re-creation of a small, 1830s New England town. Like the Prentis Store in Colonial Williamsburg, the Asa Knight Store allows visitors to experience an old-fashioned retail business in an authentic early-American setting. Unlike the Prentis Store, however, nothing here is for sale. The goods on the shelves and counters are antiques or have been painstakingly reproduced using nineteenth-century wares as models.*

In the Heart of Town

Although their potbellied stoves are mostly gone now, many country stores continue to serve as social centers for their communities—places where people gather each day to exchange views, gossip, or just pass the time. Such is the case, for instance, with the **Petersham Country Store** in Petersham, Massachusetts. With its soaring white columns, the façade faintly suggests an antebellum home in the South. Beyond the columns, however, the store is New England through and through. In the back are tables where Petersham townsfolk sip from steaming mugs of coffee and talk—often in sentences of three words or less.

"Breezy day."

"Cold winter coming."

"Fall, too."

"Yep."

Chuck Berube, who has owned the business since 1985, encourages customers to lounge at a table in one of the store's back rooms. He keeps the coffeepot full. "I enjoy the company," says Mr. Berube. "In many ways, the store is the heart of the community, and that is just as it should be."

"We sit in the back and pass around the news and the coffeepot," says Elizabeth Sherwood, a local antiques dealer and Petersham Store regular. "We've got a couple of retired ministers in our group—they pass out an occasional piece of advice—but we get all types back there. If you can't find a friend here at the store, you don't have any friends."

Mr. Berube often joins in the back-room sessions, but only when he isn't looking after customers and, perhaps, selling them some Crowley cheese. A bold cheddar "imported from Vermont," the cheese is the most sought-after item in

Seeming out of place with its columns, this store in Petersham, Massachusetts, suggests the antebellum South.

the store. "People drive here from all over just to buy a hunk of that cheddar," notes Berube. "It's so sharp it will bite your tongue off."

The store's history reaches all the way back to 1840, when Sampson Wetherell formed a partnership with Benjamin Franklin Hamilton to establish a retail business in a two-year-old building at the corner of Main and East streets. Wetherell soon bought out his partner and took over sole ownership of what quickly became a thriving general store. Wetherell ran the store for fifty-three years and for more than three decades served as the town's postmaster. To supplement his income from the store, the industrious Wetherell converted the building's second story into a small factory, which turned out palm-leaf hats by the dozen. By the turn of the century, new owners had replaced Wetherell, and the hat factory became a Grange Hall.

The store's current owner has no plans to manufacture hats, but he is searching for ways to make the store more profitable. In recent years, increasing competition from supermarkets in nearby towns has cut deeply into grocery sales. "Many other country stores are having very serious problems with this kind of thing," says Mr. Berube. "It may be that we'll have to sell more specialty merchandise— organic foods, for instance. But whatever happens, as long as I own it, this will remain a country store. Otherwise, why run it?"

Flashing a bright smile, Petersham storekeeper Chuck Berube greets an eager, young customer. Mr. Berube is the latest in a long line of Petersham Country Store owner/operators reaching back more than 150 years to Sampson Wetherell, who helped found the business in 1840.

Doctor in a Bottle

In the past, small towns often had no pharmacies—some of them still don't. Many towns had no doctors, either. Ailing folks never despaired, however, since the local general store always kept on hand a prodigious variety of patent medicines. Sick people might choose Dr. King's New Discovery, Jones' Mountain Herbs, Dr. Pierce's Favorite Prescription, Dr. Shoop's Restorative, McGill's Nerve Food Powders, McLean's Strengthening Cordial, Howe's Arabian Tonic, or any of the hundreds of other off-the-shelf "prescriptions" available. Each of these worked about as well as the rest, regardless of the illness being treated. That was because the primary ingredient in nearly every one was alcohol.

You cannot buy the above-mentioned medicines anymore. Around the turn of the century the newly formed Food and Drug Administration tested the nation's bottled and packaged cure-alls and found most to be useless or even harmful to those who took them. Congress outlawed the worst offenders, while the makers of many other remedies found they couldn't compete with truly effective over-the-counter wonders such as aspirin. Today, country stores may sell aspirin and a variety of other pain-killers or, like the Orville Jackson Store in Eagle, Idaho, stock a full line of modern pharmaceuticals; but the old-time patent medicines vanished long ago. Some folks, however, are old enough to remember them.

"No matter what you had, they could sell you something down at the store to fix you up," says an eighty-five-year-old country-store regular from the mountains of North Carolina. "But they didn't have the best medicine for you, and that was a good old jug of moonshine whiskey."

In times past rural stores offered a vast array of remedies such as those shown here. Some claimed to cure almost any ailment known to humans or animals. Most contained alcohol, some food coloring, and little else. Few could match the benefits of ordinary aspirin.

When there was no hospital or clinic, a country store could serve as a doctor's office. Here, Dr. Gaine Cannon tends to a patient seated on the counter of the Balsam Grove Store in North Carolina.

Window on the World

In the past, the title of postmaster often became a political football, even in the smallest communities. In Dorset, Vermont, for instance, the job shifted back and forth between rival storekeepers according to which party was holding power in Washington. Albert Chapman, a former co-owner of what is known today as Peltier's Market and a rock-ribbed Republican, was Dorset postmaster until President Woodrow Wilson's Democrats captured the White House in 1912. The plum then went to John Armstrong, a telegraph operator and stubborn Democrat who ran a competing store on the other side of the town common. It is said that Armstrong loaded the town's postal boxes on a dolly and hauled them bouncing and rattling across the common to his own store. Of course, residents were rarely treated to spectacles like that one in towns such as Hardwick, Massachusetts, which has only one store in the center of town.

"We know the place has been here about 100 years, but nobody seems sure of exactly how old it is," says Jean McLean who, together with her husband, Robert, has owned and operated the **Hardwick General Store** for about six years. The McLeans bought the store from Wayne and Ruth Goddard, who had been its keepers for nearly a quarter of a century. "The Goddards became quite an institution around here," says Mrs. McLean.

Situated on the Hardwick Common, a triangular expanse of grass lined with homes and churches, the store is itself an institution. Generations of Hardwick residents have stopped here to buy milk, eggs, bananas, bread, and meat—whatever they needed for the table or pantry—and to pick up their mail. As is the case in many small communities, Hardwick's general store is also its post office and has been for as long as anyone in the town can remember. For many years, Wayne Goddard served as postmaster. Neither of the McLeans have followed in Mr. Goddard's postal footsteps, but the tiny post office he ran remains in a front corner of the store. Having paid for a sack of potatoes, a cabbage, or a jar of pickles at the register, a customer can step over to the post office window and mail a letter to an aunt in Sheboygan or to the president of the United States, to a cousin in Tallahassee or to the king of Saudi Arabia.

Nowadays, all postal transactions are handled by Andrea Degan, a young United States Postal Service employee who manages the job as only a village postmaster can. Ms. Degan knows every face and street in Hardwick. Letters addressed to *Jacksonville Road* she recognizes immediately as intended for Hardwick's Jackson Road. A postcard addressed only to *Bonnie* is almost certain to end up in the proper hands. "There just aren't that many Bonnies in this town," she says.

Hardwick's Postmaster Andrea Degan knows patrons on both a first-name and P.O.-box-number basis.

A Reflection of Their Communities

When people look in the window of a country store, they see themselves reflected there. Whether it is built of adobe, wood, or stone, whether it stands at the edge of a midwestern cornfield or under Spanish oaks in Florida, whether its specialties are horse blankets, cheddar cheese, or fly swatters, a country store is an expression of the needs and wishes of its particular set of customers. Because no two communities are alike, every country store is unique.

In parts of Pennsylvania's Lancaster County, people still cling to a way of life that has its roots in small Dutch farming communities of several centuries ago. In the towns and villages where the gentle Amish gather—places with names like Intercourse, Bird-in-Hand, and Strasburg—the clop and clatter of horse-drawn buggies signal that, in many ways, these are communities where time has stood still. One would expect the country stores in such an area to be unusual, and so they are.

On weekdays it is possible to see bonneted Amish women pushing grocery carts through the aisles of **W. L. Zimmerman and Sons,** a general store in the little town of Intercourse, Pennsylvania. Often they stop and speak to one another in *Deitsch,* an old form of German mixed with a few words borrowed from English. They discuss the weather, compare prices, exchange recipes, gossip, and, no doubt, comment on the strange customs of the tourists who flock to this region in search of antiques, chocolate, and shoofly pie.

Amish shoppers fill their carts with canned goods, mixes, and fresh vegetables—many of the same items their "English" neighbors (the Amish refer to non-Amish Americans as "the English") might purchase. But there are significant differences. Part of the store's grocery section is devoted entirely to bulk foods: flour, sugar, whole-grain cereals, and other staples in ten- and twenty-pound bags. The Amish prefer to buy in bulk,

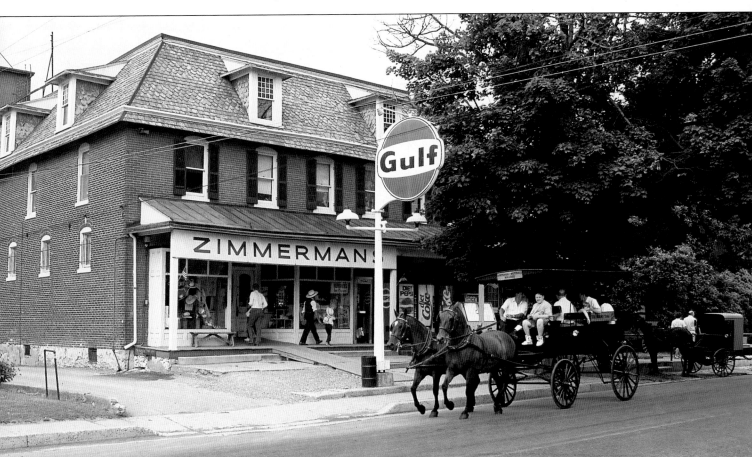

Rooted in the lush Pennsylvania Dutch Country, Zimmerman's attracts many Amish families.

presumably because it is cheaper, they have larger families, and they do most of their own baking. They eat well. Anyone lucky enough to have sampled Amish cooking knows that it is made from fresh ingredients and is extraordinarily filling and tasty. As the Amish themselves might put it, their food "eats wonderful good."

Upstairs, in Zimmerman's dry goods department, is a sight unlikely to be seen in non-Amish areas of the country. Filling a shelf along one entire wall are hundreds of black hats and below them hundreds more flat-topped straw hats with broad black bands. Amish men invariably wear such hats when outdoors, just as their women folk unfailingly wear bonnets, many of them, no doubt, made from material purchased at Zimmerman's.

In each of the ways noted above, Zimmerman's is typical of the small groceries and general stores in which the Amish ordinarily shop. Although not Amish himself, owner Peter Zim-

merman is very considerate of Amish sensitivities and traditions. For instance, he allows no cameras inside the store (the Amish dislike being photographed). Like any successful store, Zimmerman's respects the needs and wishes of its customers. As a result, business is brisk. Any sunny afternoon may bring a "buggy jam" to the parking area behind the store.

At Bird-in-Hand, a few miles to the west of Intercourse, is a business that tries to bridge the void between the Amish and those who visit only for a weekend now and then. **The Old Village Store** has been selling hardware and farm equipment to the Amish since 1890. Nowadays, however, it gets most of its business from tourists. Even so, travelers may very well see Amish men shopping in the hardware section for tools. Wooden farm and garden implements crowd the front porch. A sign posted on the front wall warns against taking photographs of the Amish who stop here.

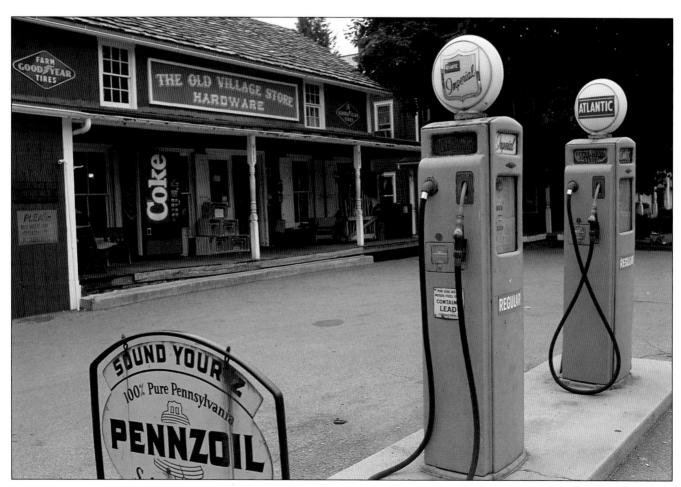

As early as 1890 this store in Bird-in-Hand, Pennsylvania, sold hardware and farm equipment to area farmers.

A few minutes by car, or a bit longer by horse power, to the south of Bird-in-Hand is the charming village of Strasburg. Buggies roll through town day and night, right past the front windows of the **Strasburg Country Store & Creamery**. Visitors are unlikely to see Amish women filling their baskets here. Nonetheless, the Creamery is filled with the rich flavor of the region—actually about 200 flavors in all. To say that this place is famous for its ice cream is to understate its reputation. The cold stuff is made in the store from fresh ingredients, most of them produced in Lancaster County.

The building at the corner of West Main and North Decatur streets in Strasburg hasn't always been a Mecca for ice cream lovers. Built in 1788, it has served as a pharmacy, post office, and tavern, as well as a general store. Today, in addition to being an ice cream and sandwich shop, gift shop, Yule shop, and country store, it is also a bed-and-breakfast; some of its eleven rooms feature canopied four-poster beds. The store celebrated its 200th anniversary in 1988 with a cake that filled half the front porch. No doubt slices of the big cake were served up with a whopping scoop of ice cream.

The Country Store and Creamery in Strasburg, Pennsylvania, is a gift shop, deli, and bed and breakfast.

Stops along the Road

COUNTRY STORE COUNTRY

Vermont

The President Who Was Weaned on a Country Store Pickle

The characteristic expression of President Calvin Coolidge was so tight-lipped that some suggested he had been "weaned on a pickle." Historians have never reached a consensus as to the accuracy of this proposal. It cannot be denied, however, that an ample supply of pickles was nearly always on hand at the country store in Plymouth Notch, Vermont, where the president was born and spent his early years.

Calvin Coolidge cried his first tears in 1872 in the unpainted ell at the back of the store rented by his father, John Coolidge, for $40 a year. As a youth Coolidge occasionally worked at the store and, as legend would have it, helped build its handsome cherry wood and bird's-eye maple counter with his own strong hands. But the boy was not to follow in his father's footsteps as a storekeeper. Once he reached manhood and had his Amherst degree, he was off to Northampton (pronounced without vowels—"Nrthmtn"—by the future president) Massachusetts, to practice law and enter politics. Years later he was elected governor of Massachusetts.

In 1920 Calvin Coolidge ran successfully for vice-president on the Republican ticket with Warren G. Harding, a former newspaperman judged by some historians to have been among the least competent men ever to sit in the Oval Office. President Harding's political worries ruined his

Vermont's Florence Cilley Store was once run by the family of President Calvin Coolidge.

health, and on August 2, 1923, he died in what newspapers described as "a stroke of apoplexy."

The sad news of President Harding's death reached the vice-president in the middle of the night at Plymouth Notch, where he was vacationing at his father's house. The older Coolidge had given up the retail business many years before and moved into a house just across the street from his former store. A conservative and tight-fisted man, he had no telephone or electricity. A telegraph operator had to drive the long, winding road from the neighboring town of Bridgewater and bang on the front door to deliver word that John Coolidge's son was now president of the United States.

Calvin Coolidge climbed out of bed, put on a black suit and tie, and crossed the road to the store, now run by an indomitable woman named Florence Cilley. The store did have a telephone, and the new president was able to reach the attorney general in Washington, D.C., who gave him the exact wording of the presidential oath of office. A while later, in the sitting room of his father's house, he took the oath. It was administered by John Coolidge himself, a justice of the peace, and witnessed by Congressman Porter Dale, a reporter, and several other men who had raced to Plymouth Notch.

It had been a sultry evening. With the oath taken, President Coolidge suggested that everyone cross over to the old store and break the heat of the night with a refreshing bottle of Moxie. (A somewhat bitter soft drink, Moxie was a Coolidge favorite.) To understand what happened next, it must be recalled that Calvin Coolidge was what used to be called a "rock-ribbed Republican" and had a granite resolve when it came to matters of fiscal responsibility. It was a simple thing he did, really. As soon as the Moxie had been passed around, the president took a nickel out of his pocket and slapped it down on the counter to pay for his own bottle—and then invited everyone else to do the same.

The **Florence Cilley Store** is still open for business as part of the Plymouth Notch Historic District, owned and operated by the Vermont Division for Historic Preservation. The store still carries pickles, and it looks much as it did in the 1920s. If they wish, visitors can sit in the rockers on the front porch, enjoy the scenery, and sip a cooling bottle of Moxie.

The scenery makes it easy to understand why Coolidge preferred the cool Green Mountains of Vermont to the cold marble halls of Washington, D.C. Being a direct man, Coolidge acted on his preference and ended up spending more time on retreat—much of it in Vermont—than almost any other president. He vacationed for weeks at a stretch in the Coolidge family homestead at Plymouth Notch and in 1924 made it his summer White House. Since the president's father continued his steadfast refusal to have a telephone, or even electricity, installed in the house, the nation's business had to be conducted from a room above the Cilley Store. That a president could run the nation from a country store as easily—perhaps more easily—than from the White House came as no surprise whatever to Vermonters.

Coolidge's staff used this room over the Cilley Store when the president vacationed in Vermont.

Without Their Pickles

The wooden beams and supports that hold up the ceiling of the **J. J. Hapgood Store** in Peru, Vermont, run off at crazy angles and come together again at odd junctions. "How all that was done is a mystery," says Frank Kirkpatrick. "We've had carpenters come in here and they can't believe it."

Mr. Kirkpatrick and his wife, Nancy, own and operate the store, which has a history just as interesting as its ceiling. In 1827 a farmer named J. J. Hapgood built a general store here. When he needed to plow fields, harvest crops, or tend to cattle, his wife waited on customers.

Peru was then—and still is—a tiny community, most of the time having no more citizens than there are days in the year. But because the village was isolated—high in the Green Mountains and several miles from any other town—most of its citizens bought what they needed at the Hapgood Store.

After forty-three years of continual operation by J. J. Hapgood and his family, the store was sold in 1870. Over the door, the new owner proudly hung a fine, hand-painted sign identifying the business as that of T. J. SNOW & CO. His impressive sign notwithstanding, Mr. Snow proved a far less durable storekeeper than his predecessor. Within a year he had leased the property to another operator, and by 1884 the store was back in the sure hands of the Hapgoods.

The old store stood vacant for a time but still belonged to a member of the Hapgood family during the 1920s, when Arthur Kelton first ran his fingers through the dust on its counters. The son of a Methodist minister, young Kelton decided he had found a sanctuary. He swept the floors, restocked the shelves, and flung the door open to welcome shoppers.

From behind his cash register Mr. Kelton watched the world change. Customers who had ridden up to the store on horseback later drove to it in puttering automobiles. Kelton pumped gas for Model Ts, for Model As, for Edsels, and eventually, even for Mustangs. He brought the store forward in time from the days of cured meat and salt fish to

Luckily, this old bucket was never used to fight a fire at the Peru, Vermont, Hapgood Store, which is loaded with history and authentic country treasures.

Now besieged by vegetable baskets, this many-drawered chest once held nuts and bolts.

the age of TV dinners. In all he operated the store for forty-three years, by coincidence, exactly the same length of time J. J. Hapgood had run it.

The Kirkpatricks have owned the store since 1977, and their success with the business surprises no one who knows them well—as nearly all of their customers do. Although he would not say so himself, Frank Kirkpatrick is an expert on country stores. In fact, he has written a book on the subject, *How to Run a Country Store* (available at the Hapgood Store or from Storey Communications, Inc., in Pownal, Vermont).

"A country store has at least one advantage over city markets," says Mr. Kirkpatrick. "It can offer more personal service and concern for customers, and people still care about those things."

Mrs. Kirkpatrick illustrates the point when a young couple rushes out of the store with a bag of picnic supplies. "Oh good heavens," she says. "Those people told me they were headed down to the pond for a picnic, and now they've left behind their pickles. What a shame."

The Kirkpatricks have worked hard to maintain the store's old-time appearance, partly through the display of artifacts, many of which were found on the property. Behind the register is a package of

Uneeda Bakers Snow Flake Wafers, a tin of Huntley & Palmers Breakfast Biscuits, and a box of Quick Mother's Oats. A cardboard poster advertises Dr. W. B. Caldwell's Syrup Pepsin: The Family Laxative, which, perhaps luckily, can no longer be purchased.

Even so the Hapgood Store is in no sense a museum. The store's' old tins, packing-crate lids, and antiques do not distract from its purpose: selling candy, soda, loaf bread, franks, and other groceries, mostly to locals.

"We get a lot of business from tourists, but we cater mostly to people who live here," notes Mr. Kirkpatrick.

"And, I'm afraid, to some people headed down to the pond without their pickles," adds Mrs. Kirkpatrick.

A Man Ahead of His Time

"NOT LUCK, BUT PLUCK," said Frank Henry Gillingham in one of the thousands of newspaper advertisements he placed during the several decades he ran his store in Woodstock. "Some of our competitors seem to think we are ruled by a lucky star." Perhaps the plucky F. H. **Gillingham Store** does have a lucky star. More than a century old and still owned and operated by the same family, the old store continues to prosper in an age far removed from the one known by its founder.

Early in the morning, when a thin layer of fog lends the town the appearance of an old photograph, it is possible to imagine that nothing much has ever changed in Woodstock, Vermont. Of course, that's not entirely true. The vintage clapboard homes and brick buildings are very old, some of them dating back to within a generation of the American Revolution. But streets that once rattled with an occasional wagon now carry a flood of more than 10,000 automobiles and trucks each and every day.

Although times have changed and Woodstock with them, the F. H. Gillingham Store continues to do business and serve customers in

much the way that it has for more than 100 years. The store still maintains personal charge accounts, still delivers groceries to regular customers, still grinds coffee beans in a red, turn-of-the-century Universal coffee mill, and still sells nails by the pound from bins almost as old as the store itself (the building dates to 1810). Earlier in this century, President Calvin Coolidge and poet Robert Frost shopped here often. Both men would probably feel quite comfortable in the Gillingham store today.

"We have customers whose families have traded with us for generations," says Jireh Billings, the store's manager and F. H. Gillingham's great-grandson. "They expect a more personal type of service, and we give it to them."

The store's approach wasn't always old-fashioned. Indeed, seen from the perspective of his own time, the store's founder was a singularly untraditional businessman. For instance, Mr. Gillingham placed his "pluck" advertisement—almost 100 years ago—to needle competing storekeepers who had taken exception to his radical, high volume/low price approach to retailing. He was among the first New England storekeepers to

When owned by Alvin Hatch more than a century ago, the Gillingham Store in Woodstock, Vermont, served customers in much the same way as it does today.

Manager Jireh Billings (above), great-grandson of the founder, holds his son—potentially a fifth-generation Gillingham Store operator. Whiskered employees Henry and Fran (right, above) assist with mousing and public relations. Toy tractors parade in front of hardware shelving that may very well be older than the store itself.

make extensive use of newspaper advertising. His ads ran every week in the local *Vermont Standard,* and he was not afraid to advertise prices, a practice many other storekeepers found shocking.

At age twenty-four, Gillingham had bought the store from Alvin Hatch, the keeper he had clerked for since high school. Almost immediately, he began to woo customers through advertisements that he composed himself. In one of his earliest ads, Mr. Gillingham laid his business philosophy before the public: "LOW PRICES LEAD TO LARGE SALES. We have determined to leave no stone unturned in our efforts to draw trade; life is

too short to be squandered in the attempt to do business in the ordinary humdrum method . . . SMALL PROFITS AND QUICK SALES will be our watchword."

Competing stores placed ads of their own, questioning Mr. Gillingham's ability to keep prices low while spending what were apparently considerable sums on advertising. He thundered back: "If you turn a dollar ten times and make a two percent profit, that is twenty percent. If you turn a dollar once and make twenty percent, that is an enormous profit."

Nowadays, the Gillingham Store rarely emphasizes volume or prices in its advertisements. Nonetheless, Mr. Billings claims he "draws inspiration" from his great-grandfather's words when composing advertisements for the store—a job for which he gets little help from the store's unofficial public relations officers, Fran and Henry, a disarmingly affectionate pair of tiger-striped mousers. Even so, the cats (whose names reflect the initials *F.* and *H.* in F. H. Gillingham) are said to handle their P.R. duties extremely well. "They make a lot of friends for us," says Billings. "They get letters all the time, and some of our customers even send them Christmas cards."

A Literary Cracker Barrel

Vrest Orton's recollections of his father's turn-of-the-century general store in northern Vermont were vivid and sensual. He remembered the bite of sharp cheddar, the colorful patterns of printed calico, the aromas of harness leather, coffee, and tobacco, and the warmth radiated by a fat stove crackling with hardwood.

Those earthy memories remained with Mr. Orton when, as a young man, he floated in the heady realm of the New York literary scene. During the early 1920s he had made his way to New York City, seeking a job with his hero, H. L. Mencken. Already world famous as a critic and iconoclast, Mencken was then editor of *American Mercury*, published by Alfred A. Knopf. The audacious Mr. Orton walked right into Knopf's 57th Street offices, announced himself, and asked for a job. Many others who had entered the Knopf building on similar missions ended up carrying their heads back to the street, having been decapitated by the razor-sharp sword of the Mencken wit. Mr. Orton, however, managed to keep his head and, to his amazement, realized his ambition of working for Mencken's *American Mercury*.

The 1920s roared for young Mr. Orton, but all too soon the Great Depression shattered his dreams, along with those of most other Americans. He retreated to Vermont and bought a house in the antique village of Weston. It was there, in the shadow of the Green Mountains, that his rich childhood memories suggested a new direction for his life. He decided to open a store of his own, one that would appeal to the senses—as well as to the old-fashioned good sense—of its customers, just as his father's business had done so many years earlier.

In 1946 Mr. Orton's memories gave shape to the **Vermont Country Store** on Route 100 near the Weston village green. Mr. Orton purchased a venerable two-and-one-half-story structure, already more than a century old, and painted its clapboard walls the same butternut red that had distinguished his father's now-vanished business. Then he filled it with merchandise that recalled the earthiness of that earlier store.

Initially, his stock was quite limited, consisting mainly of specialty items wrought in wood and iron by a handful of Vermont craftspeople, but it was quickly expanded to include thousands of traditional and practical products. Today, Vermont Country Store shoppers can buy green tins heavy with bag balm, an antiseptic salve once used primarily to soothe the udders of cows but also great for healing the dry, chapped hands of hard-working humans. They can buy Thayers Honey Anise Cough Syrup, Pickle's Healthy Feet Cream, or Dominica Bay Rum body lotion. They can buy linen bags filled with catnip or herbal moth repellent. They can buy pickled fiddleheads, Vermont Common Crackers, and crystallized candied ginger. They can buy catsup funnels, dog-biscuit cutters, ceramic pie weights, and spatulas guaranteed to lift pie wedges whole and unbroken from the pan.

An innovation introduced by the store decades ago was its *Voice of the Mountains* mail-order catalogue. Originally, mail-order purchases were packed into boxes padded with old newspapers gathered from homes around Weston. Today, however, the store uses plain paper packing made from recycled newsprint. As another innovation, Mr. Orton opened a second outlet in Rockingham, Vermont, in 1967. The newer store stands only two miles from Interstate 91, which becomes a river of tourists during the summer and fall.

Yet the heart of the business, now run by Vrest Orton's son, Lyman, remains the Weston store. It boasts a substantial history of its own by now, stretching back almost half a century. Filled with interesting aromas, it remains a place where customers can touch and taste merchandise. It is possible to imagine that, standing in the Vermont Country Store, even H. L. Mencken would have held his tongue long enough, at least, to savor a cream-filled chocolate drop.

Painted butternut red, the Vermont Country Store in Weston is a handsome reminder of a bygone era.

Packages of Pepper

Country stores have often been a shopper's last resort. Rare or discontinued items that long ago disappeared from city retail outlets can occasionally be found in a small-town general store, where volume is lower and where nooks and dark corners hide merchandise—sometimes for years.

During World War II, fighting in the Pacific interrupted the spice trade and left pepper shakers empty all over America. It is said that one day during the war years, two city women stopped at the Higgins Store in Newfane, Vermont, and happened to ask the keeper if maybe, just maybe, he had any pepper.

"Pepper?" asked Lewis Higgins. He produced an enormous drawer crammed with packets of the scarce seasoning.

For a moment the two women were speechless. Then they popped open their purses and began to stuff them with pepper packets, which Mr. Higgins happily sold them for 10 cents each. When the women had gone, no doubt crowing over their good fortune, Mr. Higgins shook his head. He turned to a customer and grumbled, "Now why in hell do you suppose they wanted all that pepper?"

Lewis Higgins died in 1961, having run his store for thirty-five years, since well before the Great Depression. Before him, Newton M. Batchelder and his brother, H. J., had owned the store since 1877, almost half a century. The Batchelder brothers had been raised near the tiny Vermont village of Peru, whose J. J.

Built in 1876, the Newfane Country Store features extended display windows.

Hapgood Store, with its interesting aromas, mysterious bottles and tins, delicious hard candies, and other delights for small boys, may have sparked within them an interest in the profession of store-keeping.

The Batchelders filled their new store with an astounding variety of merchandise. Newfane housewives could buy needles, thread, cloth, and cooking utensils there. Farmers could buy feed and seed. Craftspeople could buy tools and supplies. The brothers sold shoes, clothing, medicines, pans, dishes, flour, sugar, and, of course, plenty of aromatic spices and candy. To keep the shelves fully stocked, Newton Batchelder journeyed to Boston once every six months to place orders with wholesale houses.

Each day the Batchelders appeared at the store wearing white shirts and dark gray pants held up by suspenders. They always had a smile for their customers and usually could be counted on to recommend a helpful tonic when a family member was ill. Naturally, their business prospered.

The store the Batchelder brothers once ran has aged gracefully. In 1990, after more than 160 years of service under perhaps a dozen different keepers, it was retired from the general-store business. Known today as the **Newfane Country Store**, it is a delightful shop featuring quilts, candy, and an array of gift items almost as varied as the stock maintained by the Batchelders.

Nowadays the store sells quilts, candy, and gifts.

The Indescribable Charm of Steady Customers

"I hate to use the word `charming' because that's trite," Peter Brewitt says, groping for a description of the **Perkinsville General Store**, which he and his wife, Margaret, bought in 1990. "But there is something indescribable about this place that is—well—just wonderful."

Many of the store's attractions are obvious. It has a potbellied stove, a wooden floor worn down by generations of customers, a gorgeous location in a quaint Vermont mountain hamlet, and plenty of history, dating back to 1837. But it also has a quality the Brewitts say they looked very hard for when they began a search several years ago for a store to make their own.

"We must have looked at a hundred different places, but this is the one we wanted. It's still a functioning part of its community," Mr. Brewitt explains. "It's not an antique shop, not a gift shop, not a convenience store with a fancy name over the door. It's a general store."

As Mr. Brewitt is talking, a small boy, maybe four years old, is pleading with his father, a Perkinsville Store regular. "Please, Dad, I only want to look at the toys. You don't have to buy me one. I just want to look."

Negotiations between father and son end in compromise. No toys, but the boy does get a package of National Hockey League player cards, complete with sticks of bubble gum. He seems content.

"It's your steady customers who carry you through the hard times," says Peter Brewitt. "They're the ones who come in here in February and March and buy half a pound of hamburger."

The Brewitts sell Vermont specialty and gift items such as maple syrup, maple sugar, ciders, wines, and cheeses. "We try to stick to Vermont products," says Brewitt.

Owner Peter Brewitt (above) prepares to ring up a purchase. From across Highway 106, the old store (left) seems to have exactly what its antique sign (above left) says.

The Fifty-Year Lunch Counter

Practically the only way to get a seat at the **Townshend Corner Store** lunch counter is to ask someone to leave. "That's the way it is at breakfast and lunch nearly ever day," says Charmien Dexter, who has run the store since 1989.

Fitted with stools and covered with hard red plastic, the counter is a holdover from the 1940s and 1950s. It is the sort of place where teenagers used to fall in love and slurp sticky sodas through paper straws. An older crowd gathers at the counter nowadays, but without a doubt, most of these folks were once teenagers. In days gone by, some of them may very well have chilled their tongues on double-dip tutti-frutti cones scooped from one of the Frigidaire freezer bins behind the counter.

The building that houses the Corner Store is about a century old. Over the years it has functioned mostly as a country store, but for a time it was pressed into service as an office for the town clerk. Today, instead of licenses and tax receipts, the store once more dispenses groceries, newspapers, sandwiches, and, of course, sodas.

The Corner Store is one of three handsome old buildings across from the Townshend common on Highway 30. The other two house a pharmacy and a hardware store. All three buildings appeared in a scene of the movie *Funny Farm,* which was filmed in Townshend. Many of the town's citizens look back gloomily on the filming. The movie was shot in the fall. To simulate summer foliage, the filmmakers sprayed green paint on the leaves of the town's magnificent maples, killing many of the trees in the process.

"What a shame," says one member of the Corner Store lunch crowd.

"Yeah," adds another. "If you ask me, the people who did that belong on a funny farm."

Located at the end of a handsome row of buildings, the Corner Store in Townshend attracts a daily crowd of regulars to its lunch counter.

PICKERS
AND POTBELLIES

The Blue Ridge Mountains

A Potbelly and a Lot More Besides

The potbellied stove has always been a big attraction at the **Mast General Store** in Valle Crucis, North Carolina, a community that took its name from three streams that came together to form a cross. W. W. Mast, who ran the business longer than anyone, kept plenty of split wood on hand to stoke both the stove and the marathon whittling sessions of the mountaineers that gathered around it. He also stocked his store with an extraordinary variety of merchandise—just in case his customers wanted to buy something.

It is said Mr. Mast "hated like the devil" to turn away a customer. So he had a little bit of everything stacked on shelves, piled on counters, or sitting around in barrels on the floor. For farmers he had seed, plows, and straw hats. For carpenters he had nails, overalls, and a selection of good, stout work boots. For mothers he had cradles, and for the bereaved, caskets on discreet display in an upstairs room. And of course, for a child with a penny he always had a twist of licorice and a smile.

Although his name has hung over the door for nearly a century, W. W. Mast did not found the Mast General Store; Henry Taylor built the store in 1892. In 1897 Taylor and Mast became partners in the venture. Some fifteen years later, Mast bought out the founder and made the store his own.

As with most country businesses, the Mast Store became an expression of its owner's personality. Mast overflowed with personality—and merchandise. He sold flour, sifters, seed, feed, aprons, rope, rib-

bons, snuff, and practically everything else his mountain customers might need or want. Cured hams hung from the ceiling, and a trapdoor in the floor opened to a chicken coop in the basement.

Since there were no good roads leading into the valley, Mr. Mast struggled just to keep his shelves stocked. He traded with local farmers for chickens, eggs, meat, cheese, pickles, preserves, vegetables, and fruit. He hauled in dry goods and other merchandise by wagon over deeply rutted and flood-prone mountain tracks.

During the late 1930s President Roosevelt's WPA crews paved roads in the North Carolina mountains, opening Valle Crucis to trucks, tourists, and the twentieth century. This made it easier to bring in supplies and created a little extra business, especially in autumn, when blazing foliage attracted a rush of city visitors. But except for the gas pumps that appeared just outside the door and the fan belts displayed in a front window, the Mast Store changed very little. W. W. Mast retired in 1942, handing the business over to his son, Howard, who continued to run it much as it had always been run. But by the 1970s it seemed that the modern world of department stores,

Following in the footsteps of his father, Howard Mast (right) ran the business for more than two decades.

The Mast General Store stands up to yet another cold winter day.

supermarkets, and interstate highways had finally caught up to the old store. People drove off to bigger towns to do their shopping or left the valley for good to find jobs. In 1977 the door swung shut for what might have been the last time.

News of the Mast Store's closing came as a shock to John Cooper, a young man with a spirit not unlike that of W. W. Mast himself. An avid skier from Winter Park, Florida, Cooper happened on the store while looking for property in the North Carolina mountains, the skiing being much better there than in Florida. "The store fascinated me," says Cooper. "I wanted to look into every corner."

Rather than see the Mast Store fall into ruin, Cooper bought it and, by 1980, had reopened it.

Together with his wife, Faye, Cooper has worked hard to preserve the old-time country atmosphere of the store, now a National Historical Site. The Coopers stock many of the same items that W. W. Mast used to sell. Along with a full line of groceries, they carry hardware, local mountain crafts, shoes, boots, shirts, suspenders, saddles, and an endless selection of other "stuff."

The locals have accepted Cooper as a friend, if not as one of their own. They wink at him when they stop in to buy a quart of milk, a five-pound bag of flour, or a sack of feed. Occasionally, they still seek comfort beside the store's old potbelly, but most of them don't spit tobacco juice on it anymore.

Checkerboard warriors fight for a quarter with bottlecaps.

A pair of youthful customers
befriend a globed gas pump many
times older than themselves.
Decades have passed since the
pump was last put to its intended
use. Standing in front of the Mast
General Store, the antique gravity-
flow pump recalls an era when few
vehicles ventured into Valle Crucis
and there was little demand for
gas. Despite the ultimate arrival
of fast cars and faster times, the
store has maintained its warm,
neighborly atmosphere.

The Mast Store retains its jumbled, I-can-find-it-for-you feeling. Note the dinner bells hanging from the ceiling.

This young man finds plenty to interest him at the Mast General Store.

Banjos in the Bull Pen

As far as anyone knows, no baseball pitchers have ever warmed up their throwing arms in the "bull pen" at the **Todd General Store** in tiny Todd, North Carolina. But mountain musicians sometimes warm up their fiddles there, and local storytellers occasionally warm the ears of a bull-pen audience. Warmth is what the bull pen is all about. A sunken, rectangular area near the middle of the store, it is lined with chairs and benches and has a large coal stove at its center.

Depending on the Saturday, Todd Store visitors may feel their toes tapping uncontrollably. The banjo wizards who show up here some weekends can put a spell on people's feet.

"They bring in all sorts of instruments—banjos, fiddles, dulcimers, and guitars," says Joe Morgan, who, along with his wife, Sheila, owns and operates the store. "You never know who you're going to get."

When there is no music, an old-timer is likely to sit on a bench near the stove and fill in the quiet with stories about Todd's glory days. The Norfolk and Western Railroad maintained a turntable and terminal here between 1914 and 1936. Logging and other work kept money in people's pockets, and Todd had plenty of life. Folks who lived around here were proud to say their town had "nine stores, four doctors, and a dentist."

When prosperity comes in a flood, it often goes away just as suddenly. The Great Depression took away Todd's logging business and its railroad. Boards were nailed up over the doors and windows of one building after another. A raging flood in the spring of 1940 destroyed most of what the depression had left behind. Today, little remains but the old general store.

Ironically, the Todd Store owes much of its authentic Appalachian charm to the Morgans, who are both from California. On the West Coast, Joe Morgan had been a rehabilitation specialist, while Sheila had worked as a paralegal. In North Carolina, they are both full-time storekeepers.

Since buying the Todd Store in 1985, the Morgans have worked tirelessly to preserve and enhance its unique character. Their collection of antique Quaker Oats containers and candy boxes adds to the early-twentieth-century atmosphere. So does the circa 1910, bronze cash register bought at an auction in Hillsboro, North Carolina.

The shiny bronze cash register waits to ring up the next purchase at the Todd General Store.

Once filled with pickled eggs, cold sodas, or cure-all remedies, these old bottles and jars at the Todd General Store now serve as vessels for nostalgia.

Loafing Stools

These are discouraging times for loafers. For one thing, civilized loafing requires a decent loafing stool, something that is nearly impossible to find nowadays. But not in Hightown, Virginia. At the **Hevener Store**, which is about all there is to Hightown, half a dozen very nice stools await the world's loafers. Bolted to the floor along the outside of the oak counters on either side of the store, the stools consist of rotating wooden seats fastened atop iron posts.

"They don't get as much use as they once did," notes Jacob Hevener, the store's owner. "People used to come in—they still do sometimes—sit on the stools, and just talk." As evidence of just how much talking was done, the seats of the stools are worn to a high polish.

"People would dress up in their Sunday best, come in on Saturday night, get themselves a cola and some crackers, and just be friendly," says Mr. Hevener. "In the winter, they would gather around the [wood-burning] stove at the back, but most of the time they'd use the loafing stools."

Mr. Hevener has as good a grasp as anyone on the history of the store and its loafing stools. His family has lived here and run a general store here for longer than anyone around Hightown can remember. "Land sakes, I don't known how long the Heveners have been here," he remarks. "Since the 1700s, I believe."

This is not the first store the Heveners have operated in Hightown. Built in 1920, the present store with its loafing stools is a "johnny-come-

An inviting loafing stool

lately" compared to the log house just across the highway. That venerable building is said to be about 200 years old, and it, too, was once a store run by the Heveners.

The "new" Hevener Store was, no doubt, considered a very modern, if modest, structure when it was built a lifetime ago. For instance, it had the very latest in fire protection gear. Small brown globes containing an unidentified liquid fire retardant were hung from the ceiling at strategic points about the store. The globes were designed to shatter and release their retardant when exposed to intense heat. Almost miraculously, in more than seventy years the globes have never been put to the test. No one knows if they work, but just in case they do, the store has several replacement globes still in their original cardboard cartons.

Mr. Hevener says that the store's embossed tin walls and ceiling were once white, but time has painted them a dark cream color. Not much else has changed at the Hevener Store. For instance, the people of Hightown still stop at the 5-foot-by-15-foot post office at the front of the store to get their mail.

The Hevener Store also serves Hightown, indirectly at least, as a library. About ten books dropped off by a county library mobile unit stand on a small oak table. When people take books, they drop a signed and dated card into an empty Hershey's chocolate carton

The store's locally made oak counters and candy cases are both functional and beautiful.

Nestled in the Virginia mountains, the Hevener Store hosted countless Saturday night "loafing stool" socials.

They display a remarkable array of merchandise, including Pecos Boots, kerosene lamps, gallon jugs of cooking oil and cider vinegar, flashlight batteries, and every imaginable brand of candy bar. At the end of one counter Thomas Brothers hams lay atop cases of Diet Pepsi. Some of the store's stock has been on display a long time. On shelves in the clothing section are Bachelor Girl Budget Priced Stockings marked 2 PAIRS FOR $1.00.

Perhaps the most surprising merchandise to be found in the Hevener Store are the bottles of penicillin, kept in the cooler right alongside the canned colas. Farmers use the antibiotics to cure their ailing animals. The store stocks other veterinary supplies as well, including the small, green rubber loops used to neuter male calves and sheep. The manner of their use is not easily discussed in polite company.

Jacob Hevener keeps a "quote for the day" taped to the register. One of these is taken from the Apostle Paul's letter to the Philippians. It reads: "I have learned in whatever state I am to be content."

Not far away, written in black marker on white butcher paper, is another notice for the day. It reads: "Salt fish in #6 bucket $11.50."

Radio Flyers and Fly Swatters

If you're searching for a needlepoint fly swatter to add to your collection, the **H & H Cash Store** in Monterey, Virginia, is a fine place to look. It may be the only place.

"A friend once brought me a needlepoint fly swatter and asked me if I could make one like it," says Gailya Herold, who runs the store along with her husband, Jack. Mrs. Herold thought the swatters were a good idea, and today she makes them by the dozen, decorating them with ducks, bears, chickens, pineapples, and a flock of different songbirds. The bright red cardinals are said to be a favorite among her customers.

"I've got maybe twenty-five designs in all," says Mrs. Herold. She points to an impressive array of swatters hanging from a wire rack.

Across from the rack is another of the store's treasures: a convoy of wagons, even redder than the fly-swatter cardinals, along the top of a ten-foot-high range of shelves. There is nothing plastic about any of these wagons. Solidly built of metal, wood, and rubber, they are genuine Radio Flyers. With one of these wagons, it's easy to create a scene worthy of a Norman Rockwell illustration. All you need are a baby sister, a lazy dog, and a worn-out baseball glove for cargo, and, of course, a little boy to do the pulling.

"You would be surprised at how many of those Flyers we sell," remarks Mrs. Herold. "People remember having fun pulling wagons like those back when they were children. So now they want one for their own kids."

There has been time for at least two generations of wagon pullers since the Herolds bought the business in partnership with David Harmon in 1958. (The H & H stands for Herold and Harmon, although Mr. Harmon sold out his interest in the business long ago.)

In hopes of encouraging more cash business, the Herolds included the word "cash" in the name of their store. As with many other rural "cash" stores, however, the H & H has always done a substantial portion of its trade on credit. Boxes of customer account books fill a shelf behind the register.

Whether they pay for their purchases in cash or on account, customers find plenty to buy at the H & H. A true general store, it offers boots, shoes, blue jeans, shirts, hats, hardware, paint, kerosene lamps, feed, seed, sporting goods, and toys, in addition to the swatters, the Flyers, and a full line of groceries. Long and narrow, the store is crammed so full of merchandise that it's difficult to walk between the aisles.

Merchandise is so abundant at the H & H Cash Store that it very nearly crowds out the customers. Note the needlepoint fly swatters.

Folks in Monterey say this building—now the H & H Cash Store—has always housed a general store.

"You just ask for it," says Mrs. Herold.

A walk through the H & H reveals many delights and curiosities. On a counter near the register are large tins of maple syrup, all of it made from the sap of Virginia trees (Mrs. Herold is famous for her maple fudge). Quaker Oats, Kellogg's Corn Flakes, and other cereals float together ten feet high on top of shelves behind the register. The cereal boxes are fetched down by means of a pole fitted on the end with a rubber grip. Also up high are the trophy horns of deer said to have been shot by C. R. Gutshall, who owned the store before it became the H & H.

Below the hats are enormous bags of dog chow popular with local hunters, who keep pens full of yapping pointers and setters. Hunting is a way of life for men here in the western Virginia mountains. In a separate room that looks as if it may have once served as the Monterey post office, hunters can pick out an orange jacket, select a pair of stout boots, and thumb through a mound of denims until they find the right size. Hanging from a wire are "Seater Heaters," the insulated

pads hunters sit on to keep themselves comfortable on cold November days. According to one Virginia hunter who outfitted himself in the H & H back room, the mountains get "colder than you-know-what" during the fall season, and the Seater Heaters "are great for keeping your setter warm."

In addition to its plethora of merchandise, the H & H showcases considerable human wealth in the people who pass through its door. A visitor who listens closely might be lucky enough to hear a conversation such as the following one between Mrs. Herold and several of her customers:

"They was eighty in Bible school today."

"Well, they need it, don't they?"

"We all need it."

"I saw where somebody came to the church up in Elkins and robbed everybody with a sawed-off shotgun."

"Well, I'll never."

"Isn't that just terrible."

"Have you ever heard of such a thing?"

"Hey, Gailya, Betty asked me if you would set down a pack of Marlboro Lights on her bill."

CATFISH AND COLAS

The Deep South

A Whole Mess of Cats

In the days before producers started to prepackage most grocery items, storekeepers had to decipher an endless variety of words meant to indicate the size or volume of a purchase. People ordered a "slab" of this, a "wedge" of that, a "bunch" of those, or a "chunk," a "hunk," or a "heap" of something else. These terms could refer to any amount, but the keeper nearly always knew the family placing the order, knew how many mouths it had to feed, and so, knew how much to put on the scales.

One steamy afternoon during the 1950s, an aged customer walked into a now-vanished Southern store and ordered "a mess of cats." The keeper threw a handful of small catfish onto a piece of white butcher paper and put them on the scales.

"That ain't enough, Captain," said the customer. "I wanted a whole mess."

The keeper added a few fish.

"What are you trying to do, run my bill up through the roof?" the customer protested. "Next thing I know, you'll have your thumb up on that scale."

"Well, if you were back here, you'd have all ten of your thumbs up there," the keeper snapped. He subtracted a couple of fish.

"Now that's about right," the customer said. "That's a good mess."

This conversation did not take place in Herod, Georgia, but it might have. The tiny town of Herod is named, not for a biblical king but for an Indian chief, a famous warrior who knew President Andrew Jackson. There is a monument to Chief Herod right in the middle of town, which is hardly big enough to have a middle. Nearby is a monument of a different sort, although no less important—the **J. M. Paul Store**, where generations of south Georgia peanut farmers bought sides of beef, cans of beans, and yes, messes of catfish. It is also the place cotton pickers came to buy their lunch.

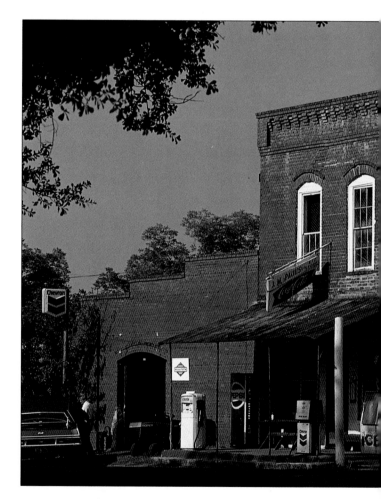

Hanging on like the sign over its door, the J. M. Paul Store now operates on a limited basis.

"People would come in from picking cotton, buy 15 cent's worth of cheese, a nickel's worth of crackers, and a nickel drink, and have themselves a real nice lunch," says retired storekeeper Virginia Paul. This was the fast-food, 1930s style. It was available to all those who had a quarter in their overalls and happened to be working in the fields near Herod.

Technically speaking, the aging brick store is known nowadays as the Herod Garage and Grocery, but the old sign still hangs outside, and most local people still refer to the place as "Paul's." That's what they've been calling it for better than half a century. More than just the name has changed at Paul's, however. "We keep bread, cakes, and candy and a few snacks and canned goods on hand—things people might forget at the supermarket in Albany—but that's about all," notes Marilyn Pope, who keeps the store open now as a sideline for the garage run by her husband, Preston. "But people who stopped off here years ago still come by sometimes. They have very fond memories of this place. It's hard to forget about a place if it holds good memories for you."

The J. M. Paul Store holds all sorts of good memories for Marilyn Pope. It once belonged to her grandparents, James Malcom (J. M.) and Virginia Paul.

The Pauls bought the Herod store during the early 1930s from J. E. Brim. "My husband had worked for A & P at one of their stores in Sumter, South Carolina," says Virginia Paul. "But when the depression came along they rolled him out. So we came here to Herod and bought this store. Mr. Brim sold it to us for a down payment of $75 and let us work out the rest. It only took a few years until the store was entirely ours."

The Pauls "did a good business" in their store. They sold hardware, farm implements, clothing, and medicines, as well as groceries. "Caskets, too," says Mrs. Paul. "We lowered them down from the attic on a dumbwaiter."

Since Paul's was the closest thing Herod had to a restaurant, crowds of truly hungry people gathered there at mealtimes. They bought sausages pulled from big jars filled with oil. They opened tins of sardines and ate them right there in the store. "Oftentimes people put pepper sauce on their sardines," remarks Mrs. Paul. "So we kept bottles of it out on the counters where they could get at it."

For those who had a little too much pepper sauce, there were jumbo-sized bottles of castor oil and a variety of stomach powders. Herod had no pharmacy, but at Paul's farmers could buy pills for their liver and spleen, tonics for their "ailing women," and powders to cure their mules of the colic.

A Little Taste of Geography

Only a few miles downstream from the point where Georgia's Chattahoochee River gets its start in White County, it flows right behind **Betty's Country Store** in the town of Helen. The Chattahoochee owes its chattering, lyrical name to the Creek Indians or, as some would have it, the Cherokees. Betty's, on the other hand, got its name from Betty Fain.

Built beside Lanier's river in 1936, the low, wooden structure has served the town as a general store for nearly six decades. The Fain family has owned and operated the store for about two of those decades, and now that their mother, Betty, has retired, Patrick Fain and his sister, Darleen, run the business.

"We try to carry things that folks don't see just everywhere," says Patrick Fain, and so they do. For instance, you might not expect to find imported New Zealand "horned" melons in a rural north Georgia market, but there they are,

just above the Vidalia onions and right beside the Fort Valley peaches and Carolina apples. "They're sort of like lime Jello on the inside," Mr. Fain says. "We heard about those melons and decided people might like to try them."

Like the horned melons, Helen is itself an oddity. By the late 1960s, Helen's commercial heart had more or less stopped beating. To get it started again, business interests sought to attract tourists by completely rebuilding the town and making it over in the image of a Swiss village. The idea sounded preposterous then, and it still does, but the transformation has more or less worked. There are shops where you can buy cuckoo clocks, cheese, and chocolate; restaurants where you can eat kraut and sausages; and half-timbered hostelries where you can get a room and find a mint under your pillow. And there are tourists—lots of them.

To attract its share of the tourist flocks, Betty's stocks a variety of imported and specialty

Betty's Country Store is known for its fresh fruit. Candy and groceries jam jars and shelves on the opposite page.

foods such as paté, and truffles. "But at the same time, we carry a full line of groceries and do a good local business," notes Mr. Fain. "We sell the best steaks this side of the Mississippi, and the sweetest sweet potatoes."

Visitors and local customers alike would agree that the half-century-old store hasn't lost its country feeling, which is palpably strengthened by the aroma of home-baked breads, cakes, and pies. "The carrot cake is from my mother's secret recipe," says Mr. Fain.

A shopper in need of a hat can buy a black derby from Betty's dry goods department. Campers can pull firewood from a large pile near the door and buy it by the piece for 25 cents. For campfire breakfasts there are stone-ground grits from the water-powered Nora Mill just south of Helen. The grits may very well have been ground by Mr. Fain's ninety-three-year-old grandfather, George Fain, Sr., who still works at the mill.

The red-and-white cooler outside dates from the 1930s and serves up colas the way they were meant to be enjoyed—in icy six-ounce bottles. Like the Florence Cilley store in Plymouth Notch, Vermont, about 2,000 miles to the north, Betty's also sells Moxie. New Englanders might have said that "it took a lot of Moxie" to turn a little Southern town into a Swiss village.

As this basket of pomegranates and the inviting doorway (bottom) suggest, country stores specialize in welcoming customers and making them feel at home.

A Doughboy's Dream

The following is a fantasy. Imagine that the year is 1917 and President Woodrow Wilson has just ordered American troops to Europe to fight Kaiser Wilhelm's German legions. The patriotic young keeper of a prosperous and well-stocked rural store locks the door of his business, joins the army, and marches off to the trenches in France. He never returns. His family is told he is missing in action and almost certainly dead. As a memorial, the family decides to leave the store just as it was the day its keeper answered the call of the drums. The shelves are dusted, the floors are swept once a week, and the roof is patched whenever necessary to keep out the rain. Otherwise, nothing is disturbed. Years pass, then decades. One generation is replaced by another. As the store's age increases, so does its reputation among collectors. Some offer large sums just for a glimpse of its antique contents, but the store remains shut to outsiders. At last, the grandchildren of the vanished keeper decide that the store's old-fashioned riches can no longer be kept from the public. To the delight of tourists and historians alike, the door is finally thrown open to the outside world.

The scenario above is not the story of the **Old Sautee Store** in North Georgia, Georgia, but it might have been. More museum than store, the Old Sautee looks as if it belongs in the Smithsonian Institution. Its old packages of soap, boxes of bluing, tins of crackers, and bottles of cure-all remedies appear to have nested on their shelves since World War I or before.

The Old Sautee Store was built sometime during the early 1880s. It operated in a manner much like that of other country stores, dispensing bread, butter, eggs, milk, and other necessities of

In a delightful, if surprising, combining of cultures, the Old Sautee Store houses a Scandanavian gift shop as well as an astounding array of turn-of-the-century country store artifacts.

The Old Sautee Store overflows with nostalgia and whimsy.

life, until about thirty years ago, when it began to run short on customers.

"When we came to this area during the 1960s, my husband and I bought groceries here," says Astrid Fried. "The store had belonged to the same family [Williams] for generations but, like so many country markets, had fallen on hard times."

Today Mrs. Fried operates a gift shop at the rear of the store, in an area that once served as the Sautee community post office. Originally from Norway, Mrs. Fried sells Norwegian sweaters, Swedish crystal, Danish cheeses, and a variety of other Scandinavian products.

At first, Mrs. Fried rented space for her shop from the store's owners. Later she bought the store itself to keep it from being sold for some other use and, possibly, torn down. The Sautee no longer functions as a country grocery market.

"But we tried to keep the front part of the building like it always was," notes Mrs. Fried.

To add to the store's authentic, old-time feeling, Mrs. Fried has scoured the countryside for antique bottles, boxes, and merchandise. Many of the packages of soap, salve, cereal, and other products that line the Old Sautee's shelves and counters appear to be unopened. The contents of some might very well still be useful. Most of these items, however, are for display only and cannot be purchased.

At least partly as a result of Mrs. Fried's efforts, the Old Sautee Store remains a venerable North Georgia landmark; it has even been placed on the Georgia Historical Register. It is easy to imagine an old soldier with his rusty "doughboy" helmet in hand stepping through the door and feeling right at home there.

Apparently hand-carved from a single log, a pair of cigar store Indians guard the door at the Old Sautee. Not surprisingly, the Indians were once used to advertise cigars and other tobacco products.

Sausage and Grits

When supper runs late, famished Florida folks have been known to say, "I'm so hungry I could eat an alligator." The meat of big Florida "gators" is not an unknown delicacy, but it is largely off limits now that the toothy reptiles are a protected species. Anyway, many Floridians prefer beef or pork.

In northern Florida, especially, sausage is a favorite. That's why hungry people so often find themselves pushing through the screen door of **Bradley's Country Store** a dozen or so miles northeast of Tallahassee. Some say Bradley's sells the "best pork sausage anyone ever cooked up for breakfast."

Now on the National Register of Historic Places, Bradley's Store got its start in a humble fashion on the homestead of an industrious north Florida farming family. Early in this century, the Bradley family took wagonloads of farm produce to market in Tallahassee, always returning with a small shipment of goods and supplies needed by the families of neighboring farmers and field hands.

Those who stopped by the Bradley place to pick up a little flour or snuff sometimes took home a couple of "Grandma" Mary Bradley's sausages as well. Seasoned with black and red pepper, sage, and salt, her sausage soon became famous throughout the county and beyond.

Frank Bradley, son of the original owners, runs the family business nowadays. Mr. Bradley has added a mail-order service to allow wider distribution of the sausage still made according to the family recipe. Otherwise, the store looks and operates much as it did sixty years ago. Sheltered by the limbs of moss-draped oaks, the store is a welcome oasis for sun-scorched travelers. The antique cold box, always filled with frosty sodas, helps take the steam out of a summer afternoon. Candy and other sweet snacks are available to fight off momentary fits of hunger.

For the truly hungry, however, the store keeps on hand the makings of an authentic Southern feast. All you need are a kitchen, a stove, and a griddle. In addition to the sausage, which can be boiled, broiled, baked, barbecued, or fried, Bradley's sells cured hams, cracklings, hogshead cheese, and, naturally, coarse-ground hominy grits. To most Southerners, a morning meal served without grits is a "continental breakfast." Southerners also enjoy grits as an occasional side dish at other meals. Astonished Northerners (read Yankees) have been known to comment that their Southern friends will eat grits even with a slice of watermelon.

Oaks spread their limbs (left) over Bradley's Country Store, located about a dozen miles northeast of Tallahassee. Although founder L. E. Bradley left his favorite chair some years ago (photo and inset, opposite page), the Bradley Country Store has continued to prosper under the guidance of his son, Frank.

Looking after the Lord's Business

The building that houses the old general store in Catherine was raised on the good earth of south Alabama about a century ago, give or take ten or fifteen years. Nobody seems sure of exactly how old it is. The walls are out of plumb and show no sign of having received a coat of paint in recent decades. The floor and ceiling sag, and the second-story porch leans precariously over the front door.

The green lettering on the tin Coca-Cola sign above the door is so faded you can barely read the words **Jim Richard's Store**. But you don't need to read the sign. As soon as you walk through the door, the owner himself will get up out of his chair by the stove, shake your hand, and say, "Hi, I'm Jim Richard."

Mr. Richard is not as old as his store but "has a few years on [him] just the same." He and his wife, Emma, celebrated their fiftieth wedding anniversary in August 1990. He hasn't been wedded to his store for quite that long, but he has owned and operated it for more than thirty years.

"One might say I'm semiretired now," says Richard, who is in his early seventies. Even so, his routine has changed very little since he bought the store in 1958. At about eight o'clock each morning, Mr. Richard opens the front door. He closes it again each afternoon at four o'clock. "Sometimes, if I feel like it, I close up fifteen minutes early, maybe even thirty minutes early. And I'm always closed on Sunday so I can go to church.

Jim Richard's Store in Alabama grows a little older every day, but from year to year Mr. Richard (leaning) and his customers notice little difference in its appearance.

You take time to tend to the Lord's work, and he'll take time to tend to yours; that's what I always say."

Some might say the store itself is semiretired now, but that would not be accurate. It still gets about the same amount of business it always did, most of it from older folks or from children, and most of it on credit. Stacks of well-worn account books fill an old Saltines cracker box behind the register.

The store has never attracted much trade

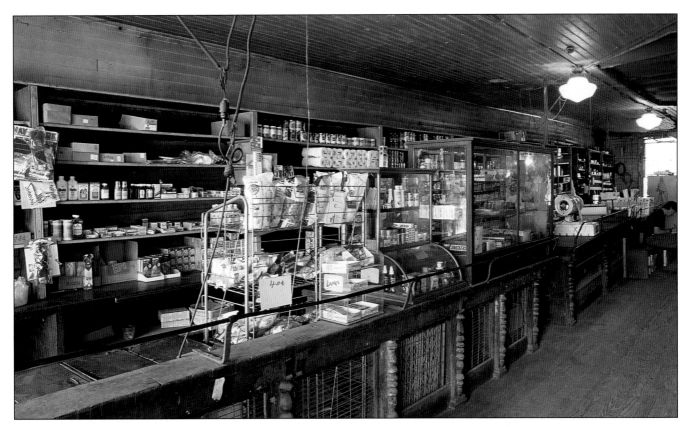

The interior of the Jim Richard's Store. Notice the iron railing running the length of the counter.

from tourists, though, according to Richard, travelers do stop by from time to time. "I've had people in here from all over the United States," he remarks. "I tell them to come on in, make themselves at home, and look around."

Those who take Mr. Richard up on his offer will see some very interesting things. Over the register hangs a mechanical string dispenser with a counterweighted arm designed to pull the string out of the way after the keeper has snapped off a piece to wrap a customer's package. Richard used the dispenser himself until all the string ran out. That was about three decades ago, a year or so after he bought the store.

Women's hose on display behind one of the counters are sorted according to size. The sizes range downward from "Big Mama."

Kerosene in a large metal barrel is hand-pumped into jugs for local customers, many of whom still heat and light their homes with kerosene.

Benches from an old railroad depot line the outside of the store's long wooden counters. The benches are an invitation to customers to "sit down and rest a spell." They are green, except where the paint has been worn through by people sitting.

Often seen on one of the benches is a man who introduces himself only as "Buster." A railroad worker who also "did a little farming," Buster is retired now and spends a lot of time at the store. Buster and Mr. Richard are old and close friends of the type who don't share a lot of talk. Anything they had to say to each other has been said a long time ago. On occasion, however, they do exchange a word or two.

"Buster, how much would you say you've eaten out of this store over the years?" asks Richard.

"I don't know," Buster replies. "A mess, I reckon."

Mr. Richard says "most all" of his customers

are friends. "These people here are among the very best folks in the whole world, just as honorable as they can be. I do business with them on credit, and at the end of the month, I cash their checks for them and they settle up their accounts. If they need help with their Social Security paper work, I do what I can. I even draw up their wills for them. Then if I'm sick or I have to go away for a couple of days, they say, 'Don't you worry about a thing, Mr. Jim, we'll look after your place.'"

The outside wall of the store, just to the left of the entrance, is patched by an aging Coca-Cola sign much like the one over the door. The sign is turned sideways and reads HENRY NETTLES STORE.

"I had a hole in the wall and asked the Coca-Cola people if they had an old sign I could patch it with. They gave me this one. I painted over the 'Henry Nettles' so folks wouldn't get confused, but over the years, with the weather and sun and all, old Henry has come back. I've decided to leave him there."

The HENRY NETTLES sign is about as faded as the JIM RICHARD'S sign over the door. It's hard to say which one will vanish first.

Mr. Richard takes pride in the office at the back of his store.

A Hubcap with Fries and Plenty of Catsup

Lunchtime brings an astonishing range of vehicles to **Cotham Mercantile** in Scott, Arkansas. The mimosa trees beside the store may spread their dainty finger leaves to shade BMWs as well as battered pickup trucks with shotguns hung prominently in their rear windows. It seems that neither the hungry local farmers, who sometimes bring their tractors to the store, nor the equally hungry gray-suited lawyers, who often drive out from nearby Little Rock, can resist Suzy Cotham's "hubcap" hamburgers.

"Those burgers are big," says one customer. "You have to eat for a while before you get to the bun."

Inside the store, business executives, veterinarians, country preachers, and politicians huddle around small tables with checked tablecloths and guzzle ice tea while they polish off hefty

Arkansas folks can shop for hardware while having lunch at Cotham Mercantile. Note the big catsup bottles.

orders of Mrs. Cotham's crunchy onion rings or fried potatoes. After lunch, if they want a Moon Pie and a cold Dr. Pepper for the road, a fan belt for their car, some ten-pound test fishing line for their reel, or a straw hat for the fields, they're in the right place. Cotham Mercantile is a fully functioning general store.

Suzy Cotham's husband, Bill, has run the store since 1958, but it has been in his family since it opened in 1919, not long after the end of World War I. It is said that some of the merchandise on the shelves is almost as old as the store itself. "When you run a store, you never know what's going to move and what's not," says Mr. Cotham.

Eager, young shoppers (right) push their money forward at the Cotham Mercantile counter. The customers below (look closely) are less lively.

Corn, Cattle, and Cash Registers

The Midwest

Ringing Up the Past

The polished bronze cash register tells the story best. It can ring up only $9.99 worth of merchandise at a time. That was more than anyone was likely to spend back in 1876 when the **Pomona General Store** in Pomona, Illinois, opened for business, but of course, times and prices have changed. "When people buy more than $10 worth, we have to ring up their stuff two, maybe three or more times," says Joe Glisson, who owns and operates the store along with his wife, Jackie Turner. "It takes a little longer, but you get the same total."

If customers feel inconvenienced by the double or triple rings, they never say so. Most of them are refugees from cities and city supermarkets. They find the clunking and clanging of the late-1800s Pomona Store register relaxing. It reminds them of a less hurried time, when paying for one's purchases was a pleasure.

The old-time charm of the store is by no means limited to its register. Its dark red paving-brick walls enclose what Mr. Glisson and no few

of his customers, as well, describe as a "living museum of American history." The register anchors one end of a nineteenth-century wooden counter lined with drawers and small windows for displaying seed. Behind the counter, cereal boxes and canned goods stand at attention along shelves that reach all the way to the ceiling. A wheeled ladder built in the 1870s provides access to the uppermost shelves, more than ten feet above the pine floors. A crank-style telephone on the wall allows customers to call in, but since it has no dial or push buttons, it can't be used to call out.

Like a letter mailed at the turn of the century but delivered only yesterday, the store is filled with reminders of times past. Tucked into a dusty display case is the April 16, 1912 edition of the *St.*

The old general store (opposite) is about all that's left of Pomona, Illinois. A sunny window brightens the Pomona soda fountain (below).

Louis Times-Dispatch, reporting the sinking of the *Titanic:* "1382 LIVES LOST," screams the headline. "868 SAVED." The newspaper is a reproduction, but the hand-lettered sign on top of the case is not. The sign politely suggests that tobacco-chewing patrons not spit on the store's enormous wood-burning stove.

The owners live upstairs above the emporium, as generations of storekeepers have before them. Both share in the work of running the store, although neither feels tied to it. When not stocking shelves or stoking the stove, Joe Glisson may be out splitting wood or helping a friend build a house. When not making ice-cream sundaes, bringing a jug of sun tea in from the porch, or selling a quart of pickled okra, Jackie Turner puts time in on environmental projects. For instance, she writes letters urging timber companies to reduce cutting in the nearby Shawnee National Forest. Thoroughly enjoying their busy, though peaceful existence—one that many might envy—the two

have apparently entered the same time warp that envelopes their store. "It feels like we've been here forever," claims Mr. Glisson.

Actually, Glisson has been a storekeeper for only a few years. Before buying the Pomona store in 1985, he was a professor of criminal law commuting more than an hour each way to his teaching job in Cape Girardeau, Missouri. But the day came when Joe Glisson put on the brakes. "I decided I wanted to live a different sort of life," he explains, "and I started looking for a way to get back into these hills."

Pomona was not always the pastoral community it is now, the kind of place city folks might think of as an inviting refuge. When the store was built, during the nation's centennial year, Pomona was a bustling railroad town with a population of more than 500. The stout pines that grew in the surrounding hills were being cut and squared off into ties for tracks, and the town was fast becoming an important shipping point for farm produce. It was a noisy time, with steam whistles blowing, locomotives chugging, and heavily loaded wagons rumbling over dirt streets. Most people had jobs and coins jingling in their pockets, some of which changed hands at the Pomona General Store.

Prosperity is mobile; it can shift from one place to another, for instance from a little place like Pomona to a bigger place like Carbondale, a dozen miles or so up the road. But small towns are rooted to the soil; they have to stay put. When the Illinois Central Railroad cleared out of Pomona several decades ago, most of the people left and things got a lot quieter. After a few years it seemed the town might disappear altogether, but it didn't. Neither did the store.

It might be said that the Pomona Store has been downright tenacious. The

original wooden structure, built when Ulysses S. Grant was president, burned to the ground in 1915, when Woodrow Wilson was president. The owners rebuilt the store, only to watch it burn again two years later. This time they rebuilt with brick, the tough, almost indestructible kind used for paving streets. Today, some three-quarters of a century later, the bricks are chipped and weathered, but the walls remain solid.

The crank telephone receives incoming calls but can't be used to call out.

Time's Ferryman

When a pharaoh died, the ancient Egyptians sealed him in a chamber with all the household goods he would need to live well in the after-world. They usually included a small but exquisitely crafted boat to ferry his spirit off into eternity. The handsome skiff in the basement of the **Stephenson & Company General Store** in Leavenworth, Indiana, was not built for a king. Instead, it was designed to carry more ordinary souls across the Ohio River. Even so, the boat is surrounded with enough antique wares to give visitors the impression they have broken into a pyramid. There are cups and plates, bottles and jugs, a harness and buggy, a cider press—plenty of stuff to keep a midwesterner happy in the promised land.

The basement looks the way it does partly because storekeeper Jack Stephenson uses it as a storage area for the town historical society. "You might say this is Leavenworth's attic," he remarks, "except that it's down here in the basement."

The skiff is an especially valued keepsake. "Dan Lyon started making boats like this one soon after he came to Leavenworth from Vermont in 1820," says Stephenson. "He used them to haul firewood out to steamboats on the Ohio."

Slicing gracefully through the river, the skiffs impressed the folks on the stern-wheelers, who began to buy them in considerable numbers. "People used the skiffs for fishing and all sorts of things," notes Mr. Stephenson. "In the old days, travelers would pull their wagons apart and load the pieces onto the skiffs. That's how they crossed the Ohio, in these small boats, with their animals swimming along behind."

Mr. Stephenson's fascination with the skiffs is fitting. For Leavenworth he is time's ferryman. In 1937 the Ohio River rose up and smashed the

The Stephenson & Company General Store in Leavenworth, Indiana

little town, which had stood for more than a century on a low-lying flood plain. The disaster proved so complete and so alarming that Leavenworth residents abandoned the entire town, rebuilding it on high ground. The community is safer now and enjoys a better view, but Stephenson feels that the earlier town, founded in 1819 by Seth and Zebulon Leavenworth, is certainly worth remembering. He has struggled to preserve its memory with documents, photographs, diagrams of the town's streets, and, of course, the memories he stores in his basement "attic."

The most revealing monument to Old Leavenworth, however, is the Stephenson Store itself. There, cake mixes and canned vegetables vie for shelf space with pots, pans, and plumber's fittings. Bins, baskets, copper kettles, and enormous crocks cover the floor. Exquisitely crafted quilts fill a fine, handmade cabinet standing right beside a metal rack loaded with bags of potato chips. Sleigh bells are suspended from the ceiling. Horseshoes hang on the wall. And what are those tins atop the highest range of shelves? "Those," says Mr. Stephenson, "are containers of embalming fluid."

The Stephenson Store continues a merchandising tradition that began in 1917, when the keeper's grandfather, John Edward Stephenson, bought the business from a local family, the Conrads. The original store, built in the 1870s, was vacated following the 1937 flood. A couple of years after the waters subsided, the present brick structure was built on a hill above the river. The new store had not been open long when Jack Stephenson, born in 1931, pitched in to help run things. "My first job was casing eggs," he says.

Since then, except for a few years taken off during the 1950s to go to college, Mr. Stephen-son's association with the store has been more or less continuous. For many years he ran it in partnership with his father, Harold Scott Stephenson. Following his father's death in 1988, he became sole proprietor.

Mr. Stephenson is always ready to try out new ideas or unusual products. For several years now he has sold the handsome products of Indiana and Kentucky craft masters: split oak baskets, hand-thrown pottery, miniature copper sternwheelers, and teddy bears with haunting, featureless faces made from worn-out overalls discarded by the husband of a Leavenworth seamstress.

In the back corner of a side room is a walled-off area fitted with a door. The room is not used anymore, but therein lies the explanation for the embalming fluid and for an interesting, six-foot-long casket kept down in the basement not far from the skiff. For years Stephenson served not only as Leavenworth's storekeeper but also as its undertaker. It was in that far corner, closed off from the rest of the business, that he prepared people for their long boat ride.

Formerly the town's undertaker, Jack Stephenson now runs the business started by his grandfather in 1917.

The basement of the Stephenson Store provides storage for historical keepsakes such as the river skiff (right). The store's main display room (below) offers hardware, groceries, and crafts. Note the chest of fine quilts and the sleighbells on the right.

Annie Oakley Knew It as George's

At almost any time of the morning, two or three residents of North Star, Ohio, can be seen sitting in one of the chairs pushed up against the front windows of **George's General Store.** They sip coffee, poured from a pot kept full and hot on a small table by the register, and they talk. Usually, there is plenty to talk about. For instance, on a fall morning in 1990 the subject was—as it often is—the local high school football team.

"That was a big win last night," said one coffee drinker.

"Yes it was, yes it was," agreed another. "The Tigers have a clear shot at the playoffs this season."

"Well, I'm glad to hear the team is winning," said a third. "But, you know, I don't go to the games much anymore. Haven't been in years. My husband used to go all the time. He would sit out there in the rain and sleet without his hat on. I believe that's what killed him."

Of course, football is not the only entertainment to be had in the area. While his customers were discussing the Tiger victory, owner Orville Niekamp posted a couple of printed announcements on the wall by the windows. One invited people to purchase $4 tickets "from any North Star fireman" for a benefit dance in nearby Eldora Park. The other urged North Star residents to let the talented Harmonizers "light up the night" for them at the Knights of St. John hall as a means of raising money to fight Alzheimer's disease.

The walls of George's General Store have been promoting causes, charitable or otherwise, for a long time. A yellowed photograph preserves the image of an early keeper, Frank George, standing beside a large poster extolling the "free silver" platform of presidential candidate William Jennings Bryan. The picture, showing merchandise piled this way and that on the counters and a jumble of watermelons on the floor, was taken in 1896. By that time, the business already had a considerable history, having been founded about 1875 by Frank George's parents, Charles and Mary Ann George.

Sharpshooter Annie Oakley, who lived less

The big display windows at the front of George's General Store in North Star, Ohio, are used for advertisements and to cheer on the local high school football team. The town's post office is attached to the building at the left.

Owner Orville Niekamp (right) enjoys a cup of hot coffee and one of the chairs drawn up at the front of the store. North Star folks use this area for gathering and gossip.

than a mile from North Star before she became a star of Buffalo Bill's Wild West Show, often stopped at George's Store to trade the game she shot for ammunition and supplies. In those days, George's did much of its business in the form of barter. Families traded butter, cream, eggs, and chickens for groceries or dry goods. To turn a cash profit, the storekeepers resold farm produce in city markets. Up to 200 cases of eggs were hauled by wagon each week from North Star to Yorkshire, where they were loaded onto refrigerated railcars and shipped to New York or Boston.

Money rarely flowed freely in rural farming communities such as North Star. That was especially true in 1934, when Joseph George, a grandson of the founders, took control of the store—at the height of the Great Depression. He nailed up posters advertising goods to be sold at prices today's customers could hardly imagine. In his "Stock Reducing Sale" on Saturday, November 10, 1934, Mr. George offered:

Post Toasties, large size	9 cents
Soda Crackers, *2 lb. box*	17 cents
George's Special Coffee	19 cents per lb.
Libby's Apple Butter, *38 ounce*	15 cents
Screwdrivers	10 cents
Hard oil in bulk	10 cents per lb.
Dr. Hess Hog Tonic	$7.69 per 100 lb.

Joseph George attracted enough customers to keep the store going right up until 1957, when he retired at age eighty-five. The business then passed to Ed Furlong and his wife, Rita, a great-granddaughter of Charles and Mary Ann George. The Furlongs converted George's into a self-service store, but it retained much of its old-time charm.

The current owners, Orville and Alice Niekamp, clerked for the Furlongs for more than twenty years. In the eyes of many of their customers, the Niekamps now belong to the store as much as it belongs to them. They keep the merchandise fresh and enticing, make sure the coffeepot is full, and occasionally put up a huge poster congratulating the Tigers on a big win. Have they contemplated changing the name of the business to, say, "Niekamp's General Store"?

"I don't see how we could ever change the name," says Mr. Niekamp.

A Mom and Pop in Ithaca

"It's rather difficult to run a mom-and-pop grocery anymore," remarks Bill Krauss, owner and operator of **Krauss's Carry Out** in Ithaca, Ohio. "But it's fun. We still sell penny candy to children. We put it in a little bag for them, just like they did in the old days."

Mr. Krauss's wife and partner, Judy, keeps the store open during the day while he is away working for General Motors in nearby Dayton. Bill Krauss pitches in when he gets home in the evening. The owners have to bring in most of the stock for the store themselves. "The bread man won't stop at small stores like this," Mr. Krauss explains. "None of the suppliers will stop here except for the beer man. He stops."

The Krausses have run their store since 1988, but the history of the business reaches back to the turn of the century. Like so many small-town stores, it was once the post office, and for years it also functioned as a depot for the electric traction railroad that ran from Dayton through Ithaca. The tracks of the line were pulled up long ago, but the old store survives because it offers shopping convenience to those who would prefer not to drive into the city. "They come in for bread, milk, beer, dog food—things they may have forgotten at the supermarket," says Bill Krauss. "We also serve a lot of older folks who don't get out much."

The Krausses say they enjoy the community atmosphere and friendliness of Ithaca. When their houses, in another part of town, caught fire one evening during the fall of 1990, some neighbors ran the store for them while they were dealing with the calamity. "They even offered to help us clean out the house and rebuild," says Mr. Krauss. "The pace is slower around here, and people have time for that sort of thing."

A cornfield stretches out into the distance beyond the entrance of Krauss's Carry Out.

Sweet-toothed Ohioans make regular runs to the **Birt Store** in New Weston, Ohio, said by some to have the largest display of bulk candy east of the Mississippi River. The owners buy candy direct from dozens of manufacturers—seventeen of them in Chicago alone. Among the hundreds of varieties and flavors are red-hot fireballs, piña colada hard candies, candy-apple bubble gum, and one-third-pound jaw breakers so large they could never fit in the mouths of ordinary mortals.

With a degree in business, Brad Birt manages the store for owner Harry Birt, his father. Both men make frequent "runs" in the store's trucks to pick up candy or the bedding plants that serve as the Birt specialty in the spring. The family business goes back three generations to Harry Birt, Sr., who established the store in 1920. The founder received an early assist from disaster when a tornado swept away all his competitors but left the Birt Store standing.

GOLD AND GRUB

The Wild West

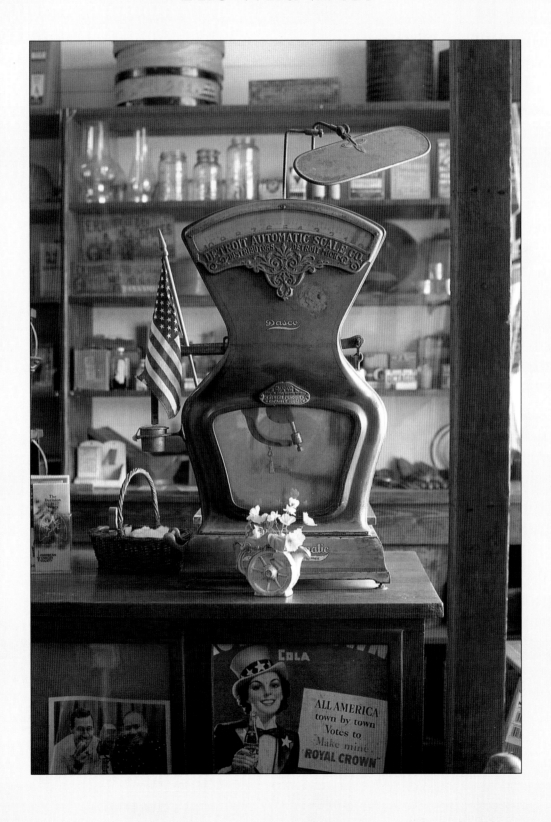

The Calico Conestogas

The story of the American country store as told in this book makes one point abundantly clear: Wherever there are customers, there will also be storekeepers. When colonial farmers moved inland from the Atlantic, wandering peddlers followed to provide them with modest amenities brought from port cities on the coast. Later, the peddlers settled down and became storekeepers. In the great migrations across the Mississippi and toward the Pacific, the process was much the same. Merchants rode in the same wagon trains that carried other settlers westward. Often they had sold most of the goods in their heavily laden Conestogas before ever reaching their destination.

Once they had found home and thrown up a building, western storekeepers often had great difficulty keeping merchandise on their shelves. Distances in the West were enormous and good roads nonexistent. Supplies had to be shipped in by wagon over rough tracks that might stretch for hundreds of miles across arid wastelands or climb through mountain passes two miles high. The likelihood of losing an entire load because of bandits or broken wagon wheels made every shipment a gamble.

Western storekeepers gambled in other ways as well. They extended credit to farmers or loaned money to ranchers who were always liable to go bust, and of course, they grubstaked prospectors. On the rarest occasions, in return for having backed a lucky miner, they might share in a big mineral strike. Mostly, thought, they were satisfied with the silver that jingled in their cash registers. They were willing to strike it rich, or at least get along, in a piecemeal fashion—by bringing a little coffee or calico into the lives of their customers.

Stores that once sold general merchandise and grubstaked Amador City prospectors now offer crafts and antiques.

German Sausage and Texas Redeye

Many of those who settled the West were immigrants who brought with them an eclectic mixture of languages and customs from distant lands. For instance, back during the days when it was a republic, Texas attracted large numbers of German-speaking farmers. It was they who taught the cowboys how to yodel and who brought to Texas the know-how for making the best sausage this side of Munich. So it should come as no surprise that one of Texas's oldest and best-known general stores has a name like *Stuermer* over its door.

In 1890, E. P. Stuermer, a descendant of early German immigrants, bought a small building and opened a saloon in the tiny town of Ledbetter. Apparently, there were a lot of thirsty people in Ledbetter. The saloon prospered, and the following year Mr. Stuermer added the adjacent general store to his properties. No doubt, he figured that operating both a saloon and a general store made good business sense. Both stood smack on the hot, dry road linking Austin to Houston, and travelers who failed to slake their thirst on general-store sodas and lemonade could step next door and banish the dust from their throats with a shot or two of redeye.

"According to Fayette County records, the buildings housing the saloon and the store had stood since at least 1870," says Chris Jervis, a great-granddaughter of E. P. Stuermer. "They had once been owned by Hamilton Ledbetter of Round Top, Texas. Of course, he was the man for whom the town of Ledbetter was named."

Mr. Stuermer added a second floor to the store around the turn of the century, but otherwise, both buildings still look much as they did when he bought them more than 100 years ago.

The saloon shut down in 1945 but was reopened again a few years ago. You can still saunter up to the polished-wood bar with its sixteen-foot brass rail and slap down a coin, but you won't be served any whiskey. The hard stuff has been replaced by frozen desserts made with Blue Bell Ice Cream, a Texas staple. And why not? Who's to say a banana split won't cut the dust just as well as a shot of bourbon?

During the four decades that the saloon was closed, the Stuermers used it to store anything and everything they couldn't sell, didn't need, or had simply forgotten about. When the saloon was finally cleaned out, it yielded enough artifacts to fill a good-sized museum: a hand-turned Elgin coffee mill, a gramophone, boxes of high-button shoes, black-powder shotgun shells, hand-operated laundry wringers, Texas license plates dating from the 1930s, dubious medicines, tools with unknown

Founded by a family of hardy German settlers, the Stuermer Store in Ledbetter, Texas, has been in business for at least a century.

functions, and countless other bits and pieces of the Stuermer past. Most of these items have now been put on display.

"There are so many memories here," says Lillian Stuermer Dyer, one of the five family members who now own and operate the store. Members of farming families who have shopped at the **Stuermer Store** for generations would, no doubt, agree. Many still remember Valdor Stuermer, who clerked at the store for more than sixty years. Some also remember a time in their youth when as many customers spoke German as did not. A few of them, though they are seldom willing to admit it, still speak a word or two of the old language themselves. And the Stuermer Store still sells plenty of sausage.

Local customers frequent Steurmer's not just to shop but to visit with friends. Two generations ago, conversation at the Steurmer counter may have been conducted in German.

Trading Blankets with Double Glasses

The way John Lorenzo Hubbell saw it, being surrounded by Indians was good business. Like most of the other business people described in this book, Hubbell made a good living by running a country store. His customers looked to him for the same everyday items that rural general stores have always provided: flour, cornmeal, sugar, canned meat, candy, coffee, tobacco, tools, knives, cloth, leather goods, and much more. Like successful storekeepers everywhere, Mr. Hubbell expected and received a decent return on his sales, but his store was on an Indian reservation and he realized his profits in an unusual and indirect fashion. Few of his customers had any money, so Hubbell bartered his wares for hand-woven rugs, silver and turquoise jewelry, baskets, buckskins, and other native American products. These, in turn, were sold to wholesale houses, jewelry stores, and retailers in cities throughout America. But to the Navajos and other tribes who dealt with him, Mr. Hubbell was more than a shrewd businessman. He was their friend.

Born in 1853 at Pajarito in the New Mexico Territory, John L. Hubbell was the son of a frontier soldier from New England who had married into a local Spanish-speaking family. A product of two very distinct heritages, he learned from birth how to build bridges between cultures. As a young man, he put that knowledge to work by serving as a Spanish-language interpreter for territorial authorities. But it was during the 1870s, when he went into business as an Indian trader at the age of twenty-three, that Hubbell's unique abilities made their indelible mark.

Because of his spectacles, the Navajos called him "Double Glasses," but it was a name they used with regard and affection; the trader had earned their respect. He helped them to understand the strange ways of white people, translating documents, explaining government policies, and interceding with officials on their behalf. He wrote

The Hubbell Trading Post in earlier times (about 1913). Note the mule at the door and the heavily loaded wagons.

letters for them, settled disputes, and found help for the sick and needy. He encouraged weavers, silversmiths, and other craftspeople to pursue excellence in their work. And he made money. Eventually, Mr. Hubbell built a trading empire of twenty-four separate posts, a freight line, a stage line, and a wholesale house in Winslow.

Although highly effective, Hubbell's business philosophy was a simple one: to treat his customers and clients "honestly and insist upon getting the same treatment from them."

The trader's sensible and humane manner won him many friends. When he died in 1930, after fifty-three years of doing business on the

reservation, the Navajos mourned his loss. One of the store's oldest customers observed sadly that "my friend Don Lorenzo is gone, and [there is] none to take his place."

Although the old trader himself has been gone for more than half a century, the **Hubbell Trading Post** at Ganado remains in business. Weavers and silversmiths still push through its doors to exchange their work for merchandise, just as their great-grandparents did more than 100 years ago. Nowadays, the store buys and sells for cash more often than it did in the past, but in most ways, it remains unchanged, looking as if it has stood on its barren patch of earth forever.

Built of wood, stone, and adobe (sun-dried mud brick), the Hubbell Trading Post seems a completely natural feature of the rock-strewn desert country that reaches into the distance in all directions from its walls. In fact, to an outsider it does not look like a store at all. Nonetheless, like country stores everywhere, the Trading Post long served as a community social center. Customers, who may have traveled many miles by horse or wagon to reach the store, tarried there while Mr. Hubbell or later owners appraised the value of their trade goods. Lingering beside the store's

rectangular iron stove, which burned prodigious quantities of juniper and pinon wood, they met old friends, exchanged news and gossip, and laughed hardily at jokes meaningless to any white except, perhaps, Mr. Hubbell.

The store sold large quantities of canned foods, which Indian customers often selected according to the picture on the can. It is said that one shipment of evaporated milk was never sold because the labels on the cans had flowers on them, leaving customers doubtful of the contents. Also popular were machine-made Pendleton blankets—ironic, since the Navajos are themselves regarded among the world's most skilled weavers. "People still buy those blankets," says a clerk at the trading post. "Every family on the reservation must own at least one Pendleton blanket. Sometimes they'll even trade their own hand-made blankets for them."

Because of its remarkable history and importance as a landmark, the Hubbell Trading Post is now protected as a National Historic Site. Operated by the nonprofit Southwest Parks and Monuments Association, the store attracts travelers and art collectors who covet its traditional native American rugs, baskets, jewelry, and pottery.

Hand-crafted baskets cover the walls of this room at the Hubbel Trading Post around 1904.

Never Just Out

Orville Jackson no longer runs Orville Jackson's. That duty has fallen to pharmacist Wayne Crosby, who bought the old drug store in 1974 from the man whose name remains over the entrance in white letters two feet high. Still, those who visit this Eagle, Idaho, landmark may imagine they can see the faint reflection of Mr. Jackson's kind face in the big display windows out front.

"It would have been very hard to change the name," says Mr. Crosby. "To tell you the truth, we never even considered changing it."

Wherever you look in **Orville Jackson's Eagle Drug** you can see the influence of the man who owned and ran the business for more than half a century. He is there in the butter churns, kerosene lamps, enamel pitchers, aluminum coffeepots, cast-iron skillets, straw hats, and mailboxes that crowd the aisles. He is there in the bolts, washers, tubing, and plumber's helpers in the hardware section. He is there in the well-stocked pharmacy. That is his motto outside over the door: YOU CAN ALWAYS GET IT OF—ORVILLE JACKSON—HE IS NEVER JUST OUT."

Born in 1893, Mr. Jackson grew up in rural Idaho, where, as a youth, he went to work for country pharmacist Allen Wilcox. Whenever Mr. Wilcox received an order he couldn't fill, he sent young Jackson racing off to nearby Boise on his bicycle to locate the required medicines. If the boy was late returning with the prescription, he

As its display windows testify, Orville Jackson's Eagle Drug is rarely out of anything.

was likely to "catch hell for it." Perhaps it was all that hard pedaling back and forth to Boise that gave Mr. Jackson the idea for the motto he would use once he went into business for himself.

Only a year or so after he returned from the World War I trenches in France, Jackson completed pharmacy school and, soon after, got a chance to run his own drug store. In 1922 he bought the Eagle Drug Store from L. B. Harris, who had opened it about fifteen years earlier in a converted grocery. It was to be the only store Mr. Jackson would ever own, and he ran it continuously for fifty-two years. Naturally, over time, it became known to customers simply as Orville Jackson's.

Over the years, Mr. Jackson remained true to his motto. He never wanted to be caught short of anything, and that determination extended not just to medicine but to all sorts of merchandise. As a result the store evolved into an extraordinary combination of pharmacy, farm and ranch supply outlet, hardware store, and gift shop—in short, a general store without the groceries.

Today, the store's personality is much the same as when Mr. Jackson ran it. Along with his wife and partner, Jane, Wayne Crosby has been careful to preserve its old-fashioned charm. But many customers still remember Mr. Jackson. Those who knew the longtime druggist well say he could "cure almost anything with one of his ice cream-and-root beer floats." It is

also said that Mr. Jackson was a faithful Democrat, so much so that, during the Great Depression, he devised his own, soda-fountain version of President Franklin Roosevelt's New Deal program. Folks with hard-working, calloused hands or work-soiled clothing were almost certain to have an extra scoop plunked onto their nickel ice cream cone. Customers with softer hands and cleaner clothes (who were therefore likely to be Republicans) usually received only one scoop for a nickel.

The Jackson Store displays its western frontier spirit.

A Bottle and a Book

Any worthy library will offer literary light—a Jack London novel, for instance—but very few of them will also sell you a 100-watt bulb to read it by. Both the novel and the bulb can be had at the **Old Fort Store** in Fort Klamath on Oregon Route 62, the road to Crater Lake. You can also buy a loaf of bread and some meat so you can enjoy a sandwich along with the second chapter. Set in the north country, Mr. London's stories cast a rather chilly spell over their readers. The Old Fort Store can help you with that also; there is coffee, of course, and the liquor department is in the back, right in front of the library.

"People make a lot of jokes about having the library and liquor in the same building," says owner and operator Joyce Magnuson. "They say this is the only library they've visited where you can check out both a book and a bottle."

According to the owner, authorities allow the state-run liquor outlet to operate in the store, a combination library, grocery, gift shop, and supply store, only because Fort Klamath is such a small community. Its population is less than 200 "even on a heavy day." The nearest town of any size is Klamath Falls, about an hour's drive to the south.

In serving a variety of functions, the Old Fort Store is typical of most other village groceries. Also typical is the fact that it has run through a considerable number of names and keepers. Built about 1910, it was known for a time as Ballou's General Store and then as Loosley's General Store. "It had been closed for a while when I bought it," says Joyce Magnuson, who grew up in Fort Klamath and has run the store since 1974. "It's difficult to say how I got into the business. I never really intended to be a general-store keeper. It just happened, I guess."

The Old Fort Store in Fort Klamath, Oregon, has a library in the back.

Dreams of Gold, Memories of Copper

The man who said "there's gold in them thar hills" did not point his finger toward the Sierra Nevadas or the Rockies. Instead, he pointed at the North Georgia mountains where he owned an already productive mine. He hoped to talk his miners out of running off to join the great western gold rush that had begun in 1848 with the discovery of a few stray nuggets in a California mill race. He failed. News that gold had been found in California set in motion one of history's most impressive mass migrations. From a few scattered thousands at the beginning of the rush, California's population quickly soared into the hundreds of thousands.

Only a few of California's fevered prospectors ever found enough gold or silver to make the trip to an assay office worthwhile. Fewer still managed to strike it rich. Some got discouraged and worked their way home, but the majority stayed on and eventually took up other pursuits. For instance, Samuel Clemens—known to generations of readers as Mark Twain—tried prospecting in the California gold fields but soon grew tired of the drudgery. Clemens then turned to journalism because, as he put it, he "could not find honest work."

Between 1848 and 1860 as many as 500 towns sprang up in or near gold country. In time, most would sink back into the soil or mine tailings on which they had been raised. One that did not was Sheridan, founded in 1855 at a junction of wagon roads. The town had an advantage in that mining was never really the reason for its existence. Known originally by the name of Union Shed, it had a large, enclosed building where wagon teams could be corralled for the night. Before long, it also boasted a post office, a bank, a

The Sheridan Country Store in California has been a focus of controversy. Developers want to pull it down to make room for a modern structure.

hotel, a flour mill, and a variety of stores. Toward the end of the 1860s, the proud citizens renamed their town after Philip Sheridan, the hard-fighting Civil War general, as an adjacent town had already been named after President Lincoln.

Among those most likely to make money from the gold rush were the storekeepers who sold supplies to the miners. In some areas where there had been lucrative strikes, a hunk of bread might go for $1 and a shovel for as much as $20. Since there were no big strikes near Sheridan, however, its storekeepers were probably a good deal more scrupulous. From what little is known of John Ziegenbein, the owner of Sheridan's first general store, he was no price gouger but rather a straightforward and prudent businessman who also owned prosperous stores in neighboring Lincoln and Daneville. Mr. Ziegenbein established the Sheridan Store in 1868, but by 1875 he had passed it along to Walter Nuestadt and moved to San Francisco.

An ambitious man, Mr. Neustadt placed showy notices in the Auburn, California, *Placer Herald,* advertising an amazing variety of merchandise. In one advertisement, he listed stock including "Groceries, Provisions, Tobacco, Cigars, Liquors, Medicines, Drugs, Paints, Oils, Cutlery, Hardware, Wallpaper and Carpets, Agricultural Implements, Lime, Crockery, Clothing, Dry-Goods, Boots & Shoes, Stationery, Fancy Notions, Garden Seeds, Flour and Mill Feed, Stoves and Tinware." Like other storekeepers of the period, Mr. Neustadt bought some produce directly from local farmers and ranchers. In the same notice he offered to "Pay the Highest Cash Price for Wool and Hay, Hides, Tallow, Butter, Poultry, Eggs, Stoves & four foot wood." At the end of the advertisement, the keeper reminded customers that his store served Sheridan as a post office and Wells Fargo office.

In spite of the breadth of his offerings, Mr. Neustadt went bust. Running a small business in frontier California was hard, and later keepers often suffered the same unhappy fate. But the store itself always survived the misfortune of its owners.

The dry California air tends to wring the moisture out of wooden buildings and turn them into fire traps. With this in mind, builders gave the store brick walls and heavy iron fire doors. A little more than a decade after the doors first opened, these precautions proved their value when a disastrous fire swept through the Sheridan commercial district. When the last embers began to cool, only the Sheridan Store remained standing.

Ten more decades have passed since the big Sheridan fire, and the old market, known nowadays as the **Sheridan Country Store,** has survived countless other calamities. Storms, earthquakes, and later fires have not been able to bring it down. Neither have recessions, depressions, business failures, and at least three cars that have careened off California 65 and into its walls. Sheridan natives can still buy a sack of flour, a bag of candy, or a bar of soap in a store where their grandparents may once have shopped for those same items. Unfortunately, this pleasure may not be available for much longer. The old Sheridan Store is in trouble.

The vintage building has passed through the hands of several owners in recent years, more than one of whom wanted to tear it down. But the wrecking cranes and bulldozers have not yet arrived. Each time they threaten, a coalition of local residents and historical organizations rush to the offices of Placer County zoning officials to block the way.

If he had lived in the 1990s, would Mr. Neustadt have wanted to see the Sheridan Store saved? It's hard to say. He learned the hard way that stores have cash registers for a reason—they exist to make money. But they also exist for people. Every country store is a monument to the struggles, victories, and travails of those who have run it, those who have depended on it for cornmeal and bacon, and those who have only warmed themselves by its stove. That makes them wonderful places to prospect for memories. Yet, we push through their screen doors not so much for history as for refreshment—and to see what we can buy for just a penny.

APPENDIX

Appendix

The following list provides basic information on the forty-six country stores profiled in this book and includes a number of additional stores of note. All of the listed stores are worth a visit—just as are countless others. This list represents, in other words, only a tiny sampling of the thousands of charming retail businesses that stand along America's back roads, waiting for you to discover them.

A word of caution: Some of the stores listed below are difficult to find. Always have plenty of gas in the car and take along a good map. Also, since hours may change from day to day and season to season, it may be best to call before you visit.

Alabama

Harrison Brothers Store, 124 South Side of Square, Huntsville, AL 35801; (205) 536–3631. Established in 1879. Sells hardware, gifts, and old-time merchandise; features antique fixtures and old-fashioned atmosphere; now operated by the Huntsville Historic Foundation. Located on the south side of the town square in downtown Huntsville.

Jim Richards' Store, P.O. Box 39, Catherine, AL 36728; (205) 225–4411. Established at turn of the century. Sells groceries and general merchandise; truly a relic of another era. Located just off Route 5 in Catherine.

Arizona

Hubbell Trading Post National Historic Site, P.O. Box 150, Ganado, AZ 86505; (602) 755–3475. Established in 1876. Sells native American jewelry, baskets, and hand-woven rugs as well as groceries and general merchandise; historic building features stone and adobe architecture and some of the finest art and crafts to be found in the Southwest. Located about one mile west of Ganado on the Navajo Indian Reservation off Route 264 (Navajo Route 3).

Arkansas

Cotham Mercantile, Route 1, Box 1, Scott, AR 72142; (501) 961–9284. Established in 1919. Sells groceries and general merchandise, serves lunch; people drive out from Little Rock (about eight miles away) to enjoy the hamburgers and onion rings. Located on Route 161.

Gilbert General Store, P.O. Box 45, Gilbert, AR 72636; (501) 439–2386. Established in 1901. Sells groceries, gifts, and general merchandise. Located on Route 333 about three miles off U.S. 65 in Gilbert.

California

Sheridan Country Store, 5780 13th Street, Sheridan, CA 95681; (916) 633–2123. Established in 1869; present structure built in 1879. Sells groceries, gifts, and specialties. Located on access road adjacent to Route 65 in Sheridan.

Sherrills Antiques, P.O. Box 184, Amador City, CA 95601; (209) 267–5578. Built in 1878 after fire destroyed much of the town. Now an antiques business, once a general store that served prospectors and gold miners. Located just off Route 49 in Amador City.

Victorian Closet, P.O. Box 141, Amador City, CA 95601; (209) 267–5250. Built in 1878. Now a vintage clothing and antiques business, once a saloon and a restaurant serving the gold-rush community. Located on Route 49 in Amador City.

Connecticut

North Woodstock Country Store, Star Route 169, East Woodstock, CT 06231; (203) 928–4117. Dates from the turn of the century. Sells gifts, groceries, and deli foods. Located on Route 169 near Woodstock.

Woodstock Stand, Route 169, Woodstock, CT 06231; (203) 928–7332. Sells fruits, vegetables, cheeses, barbecued chicken, gourmet gift baskets, and "udderly fantastic" ice cream. Located near the intersection of Route 169 and Joy Road.

Florida

Bradley's Country Store, Route 3, P.O. Box 610, Tallahassee, FL 32308; (904) 893–1647. Built in 1927. Specializes in country smoked and fresh sausage; also well known for its "cracklins," grits, and cornmeal. Located about twelve miles northeast of Tallahassee on the Centerville Road.

Evinston General Store, Evinston, FL 32633; (904) 591–1334. Established in 1882. Sells crafts, specialty items, and general merchandise. Located on County Road 225 beside U.S. 441 in Evinston (south of Gainsville).

McIntosh General Hardware, McIntosh, FL 32664; (904) 591–2028. Established at turn of the century. Sells hardware, general merchandise, and antiques. Located off U.S. 441 in McIntosh.

Oldest Store Museum in America, 4 Artillery Lane, St. Augustine, FL 32084; (904) 829–9729. Authentic turn-of-the-century store museum containing more than 100,000 vintage artifacts. Located in the historic district of St. Augustine.

Georgia

Betty's Country Store, P.O. Box 599, Helen, GA 30545; (404) 878–2943. Established in 1936. Sells groceries, gourmet foods, gifts, and general merchandise; well known for its fresh fruit, shipped in from as far away as New Zealand. Located on Route 75 at the north end of Helen.

A dog meets his best friend outside the Gilbert General Store near Arkansas' scenic Buffalo River.

J. M. Paul Store (Herod Garage and Grocery), P.O. Box 138, Dawson, GA 31742; (912) 995–5236. Established at turn of the century. Sells snacks, candy, soft drinks, cakes, bread, and a few canned goods. Located on Route 55 in Herod, a few miles south of Dawson.

Nora Mill and Store, P.O. Box 599, Helen, GA 30545; (404) 878–2375. At least 100 years old. Sells gifts, fresh-baked goods, and stone-ground flours from the adjacent water mill, which is open to the public. Located on Route 75 about one mile south of Helen.

Old Sautee Store, Sautee, GA 30571; (404) 878–2281. Dates to 1870s. Sells Scandinavian gifts; features many one-of-a-kind antiques and country-store artifacts. Located on Route 17 in Sautee.

Idaho

Orville Jackson's Eagle Drug, P.O. Box 398, Eagle, ID 83616; (208) 939–6511. Established in 1906, it is one of the oldest drug stores in the West. Offers a full-service pharmacy and sells hardware, horse tack, and general merchandise. Located on Route 44 in Eagle, a few miles west of Boise.

Illinois

Pomona General Store, Pomona, IL 62975; (618) 893–2997. Established in 1876; burned and rebuilt in 1917. Sells groceries, gifts, ice cream, and deli sandwiches served with pickled okra; features an authentic old-fashioned ambience. Located in Pomona about one mile off Route 127.

Indiana

Birkla Store, Route 66 South, Sulphur, IN 47174; (812) 843–5814. Established about 100 years

Oak storage bins at the Nora Mills Store, which serves mostly as a gift shop

ago. Sells groceries, boots, sporting goods, feed, and general merchandise; visitors may feel they have been thrown back in time to the 1930s. Located on Route 66 South, a few miles south of Route 62.

Stephenson & Company General Store, P.O. Box 127, Leavenworth, IN 47137; (812) 739–4242. Established in 1917; rebuilt in 1939. Sells groceries, hardware, crafts, and primitive antiques; the stock is extraordinary and delightful, including such items as honeysuckle baskets, hand-crafted wooden toys, and sleigh bells. Located just off Route 62 in Leavenworth.

Iowa

Living History Farms, Walnut Hills, IA (near Des Moines); for information call (515) 278–2400. A large-scale living history museum consisting of several farms depicting Iowa farm life from Indian times to the present; among the display buildings is an 1870s general store staffed by costumed interpreters. Take exit 125 off Interstate 80 and follow U.S. 6 to the entrance.

Kansas

Yoder Hardware, Main Street, Yoder, KS 67585; (316) 465–2277. Established at turn of the century. Sells hardware and general merchandise; features old-time atmosphere; many Amish families live in the area and shop here. Located off Route 96 in Yoder.

Kentucky

Carris's Grocery, Route 4, Shelbyville, KY 40065; (502) 738–5163. Established in 1882; this building constructed in 1915. Sells groceries and snacks. Located at intersection of routes 53 and 714.

Maine

Frisbee's Store, 88 Pepperrell Road, Kittery Point, ME 03905; (207) 439–0014. Established in 1828 and has remained in the Frisbee family ever since. Sells groceries, meats, and general merchandise. Located on Pepperrell Road, Route 103 in Kittery Point.

Merrill Hinckley, Blue Hill, ME 04614; (207) 374–2821. Sells groceries, meats, imported foods, liquor, wine, and beer; features an old-time coastal Maine atmosphere. Located just off Route 15 in Blue Hill.

Massachusetts

Hardwick General Store, On the Common, Hardwick, MA 01037; (413) 477–6912. Established about 100 years ago. Sells groceries and features a full-service post office. Located on a quaint town common just off Route 32A.

Asa Knight Store (in Old Sturbridge Village), 1 Old Sturbridge Village Road, Sturbridge, MA 01566; (508) 347–3362. Established during the 1830s in Dummerston, Vermont, the Knight Store closed in 1863. Today it is part of Old Sturbridge Village, a living history museum where New England village life of 150 years ago is re-created; the store's antique or faithfully reproduced wares are not for sale. Old Sturbridge Village is located just off U.S. 20 (near Interstates 84 and 90) in Sturbridge.

Petersham Country Store, Petersham, MA 01366; (508) 724–3245. In operation since 1840; the building dates to 1838. Sells groceries and gifts; specialties include maple syrup, maple candies, and cheddar cheese that is "bite-your-tongue" sharp; features unusual architecture and antique fixtures. Located on Route 32 in Petersham.

Mississippi

Old Country Store (Cohn Brothers), P.O. Box 217, Lorman, MS 39096; (601) 437–3661. Established in 1875; building dates from 1890. Sells groceries and general merchandise. Located off Route 61 north of Natchez.

Taylor Grocery, P.O. Box 66, Taylor, MS 38673; (601) 236–1716. Dates to 1910. Sells groceries and general merchandise; also serves catfish—some say the best in the country. Many say this was the model for the country stores that frequently appeared in the novels of William Faulkner. Located about ten miles south of Oxford on Old Taylor Road.

Montana

Virginia City General Store, Box 338, Virginia City, MT 59755; (406) 843–5377. Buildings in historic area date to the Montana gold-rush era (1863 and after). General store serves as a museum. Located on Montana Route 287 (off U.S. 287).

New Hampshire

Mohawk General Store, Box 157, Lochmere, NH 03252; (603) 524–7766. An abandoned railroad depot was moved to this site and opened as a store in 1938. The sign outside says ICE CREAM, FRUITS, VEGETABLES, TONIC, CIGARS, TOBACCO, CANDY. Sells groceries, beer, wine, and fishing tackle. Located on U.S. 3 in Lochmere.

New York

Ancramdale General Store, Route 8, Ancramdale, NY 12503; (518) 329–2767. Established at turn of the century. Sells groceries and gifts. Located off Route 82.

North Carolina

Mast General Store, Valle Crucis, NC 28691; (704) 963–6511. Dates to 1892. Sells groceries, gifts, and general merchandise; if you could visit only one country store, this would be the one to see. Located on Route 194 in Valle Crucis.

Old Hampton Store, P.O. Box 57, Linville, NC 28646; (704) 733–5213. Established at turn of the century. Sells general merchandise plus corn-meal and grits ground daily at the adjacent gristmill. Off 221 bypass near Linville.

Rickman's Store, 25 Cowee Creek Road, Franklin, NC 28734; (704) 524–2223. About 100 years old; owned and operated by Tom Rickman since 1924. Sells groceries and general merchandise. Located off Highway 28 north of Franklin.

Rockford General Store, Route 2, Dobson, NC 27017; (704) 374–5317. About ninety years old. Sells bulk candy, gifts, and country crafts; features a country-store sign shop. Located on Rockford Road off Route 601 (follow signs to Rockford).

Todd General Store, Todd, NC 28684; (919) 877–1067. Established at turn of the century. Sells groceries, gifts, and general merchandise; features a "bull pen" with a wood-burning stove. Located in Todd on Railroad Grade Road (County Road 1100).

North Dakota

Fort Union Trading Post, Route 3, P.O. Box 71, Williston, ND 58801; (701) 572–9083. Dates to the 1850s. Functions as a museum but no longer operates as a store or trading post. Located at the Fort Union Trading Post National Historic Site southwest of Williston, North Dakota.

Ohio

Birt Store, Main Street, New Weston, OH 45348; (513) 338–3111. Established in 1920. Sells groceries, gifts, and general merchandise; offers one of the largest stocks of bulk candies seen anywhere. Located just off Routes 118 and 705 in New Weston.

Coleman's Store, Gratis, OH 45330; (513) 787–3413. Dates to 1940s. Sells groceries and general merchandise; specializes in handmade wooden toys. Located on Route 503 in Gratis.

George's General Store, 4 South Main Street, North Star, Ohio 45350; (513) 336–7341. More than 100 years old. Sells groceries and hardware; fully stocked and immaculately kept. Located on U.S. 127 in North Star.

Krauss's Carry Out, 6667 Cross Street, Ithaca, OH 45304; (513) 678–9800. About 100 years old. Small grocery market in a bucolic setting. Located off Route 503 in Darke County.

Oregon

Frenchglen Mercantile, Frenchglen, OR 97736; (503) 493–2565. Established at turn of the century. Sells groceries, gifts, and general merchandise; surrounded by pristine wilderness. Located on Route 205 adjacent to Malheur National Wildlife Refuge.

Old Fort Store, P.O. Box 534, Fort Klamath, OR 97601; (503) 381–2345. Dates to 1910. Sells groceries and general merchandise; the back of the store serves as the community library. Located off Route 62 south of Crater Lake National Park.

Pennsylvania

Kauffman's Hardware, P.O. Box 136, New Holland, PA 17557; (717) 354–4606. In business continuously since 1779, this is one of the oldest country stores in the United States. Sells hardware and general merchandise. Located on Route 23 in New Holland.

Old Village Store, Route 340, Bird-in-Hand, PA 17505; (717) 397–1291. Established at turn of the century. Sells hardware, gifts, souvenirs, and crafts typical of the Pennsylvania Dutch Country. Located on Route 340 in Bird-in-Hand.

Strasburg Country Store & Creamery, 1 West Main Street, Strasburg, PA 17579; (717) 667–0766. Built in 1788. Famous for its homemade ice cream, the store also sells deli sandwiches, teas, coffees, penny candies, and country wares; the building contains an elegant bed-and-breakfast. Located on Route 741 in the center of Strasburg.

W. L. Zimmerman and Sons, 3601 Old Philadelphia Pike, Intercourse, PA 17534; (717)

768–8291. Established at turn of the century. Sells groceries and general merchandise; old-fashioned Dutch Country market frequented by Amish families. Located on Route 340 in Intercourse.

South Carolina

Cuzzins General Store, 7059 Highlands Highway, Mountain Rest, SC 29664; (803) 638–6627. Dates to early twentieth century. Sells groceries, gifts, mountain crafts, and general merchandise; mountain musicians frequently gather for guitar and banjo-picking sessions outside this South Carolina landmark. Located near the intersection of routes 28 and 107.

Tennessee

Cumberland General Store, Route 3, P.O. Box 81, Crossville, TN 38555; (615) 484–8481. Opened in 1973. Sells hardware, general merchandise, country hams, and much more. Located on U.S. 127, just south of Crossville.

Texas

Bergheim General Store, P.O. Box 58, Bergheim, TX 78004; (512) 336–2112. Built in 1903. Sells groceries and general merchandise; still operated by the same family that founded the business; features unusual stone construction. Located ten miles east of Boerne on Route 46.

Farmer's Mercantile, P.O. Box 782, Orange, TX 77630; (409) 883–2941. Opened in 1928. Sells general merchandise; still stocks many of the same items that were on its shelves sixty years ago. Located at 702 West Division Street in Orange (off Interstate 10 near the Louisiana border).

Lajitas Trading Post, Star Route 70, P.O. Box 436, Terlingua, TX 79852; (915) 424–3234. Established in late 1800s. Sells groceries and general merchandise; situated on the border of Mexico, it features authentic western atmosphere. Located off Route 170 in Lajitas, near Big Bend National Park.

The Cumberland General Store in Tennessee

P. Lesser and Son, P.O. Box 13, Chappell Hill, TX 77426; (409) 836–5756. Dates to 1876. Sells dry goods, hardware, smoked sausage, and much more. Located on Main Street in Chappell Hill, off U.S. 290.

T. C. Lindsey & Company General Store, P.O. Box 34, Jonesville, TX 75659; (903) 687–3382. Opened in 1847, only two years after Texas was admitted as a state. Sells groceries, feed, and dry goods; the store has been used as a setting for six different movies. Located on Route 134 in Jonesville, about fifteen miles from Marshall.

McNeil Post Office and General Store, McNeil, TX 78651; (512) 255–8330. Dates to 1862; the post office opened in 1882 and has had only six postmasters since then. Sells groceries and general merchandise. Located off Burnet Road near Round Rock.

Old Camp Verde General Store, P.O. Box 69, Camp Verde, TX 78010; (512) 634–7722. Established in 1857, but this building dates from the turn of the century. Sells general merchandise; the store originally served the U.S. Army post set up in 1856 by then-Secretary of War Jefferson Davis (later president of the Confederacy) as a facility to test the use of camels by the military. Located on Route 173 south of Kerrville.

Stuermer Store, P.O. Box 212, Ledbetter, TX 78946; (409) 249–5642. About 100 years old. Sells groceries, general merchandise, sandwiches, and ice cream; features an extraordinary array of merchandise, some of it dating from the turn of the century. Located at the intersection of U.S. 290 and Farm-to-Market Road 1291 in Ledbetter.

Telegraph Store, P.O. Box 3, Telegraph, TX 76883; (915) 446–2284. Dates to 1895. Sells groceries and general merchandise; serves as post office for the tiny town of Telegraph in the sheep-ranching country west of San Antonio. Located on U.S. 377 south of Junction.

Vermont

Florence Cilley Store, Plymouth, VT 05056; (802) 672–3773. The building dates from about 1870 but was extensively remodeled in 1890. Sells old-fashioned candy, gifts, Vermont foods, and souvenirs; open daily late May to mid-October; this is the store where President Calvin Coolidge was born. Located just off Route 100A in Plymouth Notch Village.

F. H. Gillingham Store, Woodstock, VT 05091; (802) 457–2100 or (800) 344–6668 for mail order. Established in 1886. Sells groceries, gifts, hardware, and gardening supplies; run by the same family for more than a century, this vintage store still does business the old-fashioned way. Located on Elm Street in Woodstock.

Grafton Village Store, Grafton, VT 05146; (802) 843–2348. Established in 1841. Sells groceries, gifts, and deli sandwiches. Located in the immaculately restored village of Grafton on Route 121.

J. J. Hapgood Store, P.O. Box 117, Peru, VT 05152; (802) 824–5911. Established in 1827. Sells groceries, gifts, and candy; the architecture is extraordinary, especially inside; owner Frank Kirkpatrick is quite knowledgeable about the country-store business and has written a couple of books on the subject. Located in Peru just off Route 30.

Newfane Country Store, Route 30, P.O. Box 56, Newfane, VT 05345; (802) 365–7007. Built in 1876 on the site of the old Jones Exchange Building, which had burned two years earlier. Sells candy, gifts, and crafts. Located in Newfane on Route 30.

Peltier's Market, Church Street, Dorset, VT 05251; (802) 867–2284. Established in 1816. One of the most beautiful and best-run traditional country stores anywhere. Sells groceries, candy, fresh bakery goods, gourmet foods, and an excellent selection of wines. Located on the Dorset Common just off Route 30.

Perkinsville General Store, Route 106, Perkinsville, VT 05151; (802) 263–5474. Established in 1837. Sells groceries and Vermont specialties. Located on Route 106 in Perkinsville.

South Woodstock Country Store, South Woodstock, VT 05071; (802) 457–3050. Dates from the nineteenth century. Sells groceries and gifts; has an impressive dark red exterior; pumpkins cover the porch in fall. Located at a sharp bend of Route 106, about eight miles south of Woodstock.

Townshend Corner Store, P.O. Box 152, Townshend, VT 05353; (802) 365–4624. About 100 years old. Sells groceries and gifts, but the biggest attraction here is the lunch counter, where local folks gather to jaw—the ice cream and sandwiches are delicious. Located on Route 30, across from the common in Townshend.

Vermont Country Store, Route 100, Weston, VT 05161; (802) 824–3184. Founded in 1945. Sells natural fiber clothing, kitchenware, candy, crackers, cheese, and old-fashioned specialties; merchandise can also be ordered through the store's *Voice of the Mountains* catalogue. Located on Route 100 in the astonishingly picturesque village of Weston.

Vermont Country Store (Rockingham), R.R. 1 Box 177B, Bellows Falls, VT 05101; (802) 463–2224. Opened in 1967 as a companion to Weston operation; stock is much the same as at the Weston store. Located on the access road from Route 103 in Rockingham.

West Townshend Country Store, P.O. Box 62, West Townshend, VT 05359; (802) 874–4906. Established in 1848, it is said to be the oldest *continuously* operating general store in Vermont. Sells groceries, gifts, deli sandwiches, and ice cream. Located on Route 30, about five miles northwest of Townshend.

H. N. Williams General Store, Dorset, VT 05251; (802) 867–5353. Established in 1840. An unusual and spectacular store with an astounding array of merchandise. Located on Route 30, about half a mile south of Dorset Village.

Virginia

Hackley's General Merchandise, P.O. Box 75, Amissville, VA 22002; (703) 937–5373. Dates to the turn of the century. Sells groceries and general merchandise. Located off U.S. 211 in Amissville (near Warrenton).

Hevener Store, Hightown, VA 24444; (703) 830–1230. Present building dates to 1920. Sells groceries and general merchandise; features loafing stools and a wood-burning stove. Located in Hightown about six miles west of Monterey on U.S. 250.

Early October at the South Woodstock Country Store in Vermont

H & H Cash Store, P.O. Box 172, Monterey, VA 24465; (703) 468–2570. Dates to the turn of the century. Sells maple syrup, maple sugar, groceries, hardware, sporting goods, clothing, shoes, and "practically anything else you are likely to need"; features high shelves, a fantastic jumble of merchandise, and an authentic country atmosphere. Located on U.S. 250 in Monterey.

Laurel Mills Store, Route 1, Box 176, Castleton, VA 22716; (703) 937–3015. Established in 1877. Sells antiques, gifts, and groceries. Located in Rappahannock County off routes 729 and 618, south of U.S. 211.

Mayberry Trading Post, Route 602, Meadows of Dan, VA 24120; (703) 952–2155. Dates to 1892. Sells groceries, gifts, and general merchandise. Located on Route 602 near the Blue Ridge Parkway, about four miles south of the scenic Mabry Mill.

Miller's Store, Head Waters, VA 24442; (703) 396–6184. Established at turn of the century. Sells groceries and general merchandise as well as hunting and fishing licenses. Located on U.S. 250, about forty minutes west of Staunton.

Prentis Store, P.O. Box C, Williamsburg, VA 23187; (800) HIS–TORY. Opened for business in 1740. Sells gifts and crafts; operates as part of Colonial Williamsburg; the store's stock is much the same as in the eighteenth century. On Duke of Gloucester Street in Colonial Williamsburg.

Sugar Tree Country Store, P.O. Box 19, McDowell, VA 14458; (703) 396–3469. Built about 1870. Sells antiques, gifts, and Virginia maple syrup; operated as a general store until the late 1960s. Located just off U. S. 250 in McDowell.

Wolftown Cash & Carry, Wolftown, VA 22748; (703) 948–6635. Dates to the early twentieth century. Sells groceries and general merchandise; houses the community post office. Located on Route 230 in Wolftown.

Wolftown Mercantile Country Store, Wolftown, VA 22748; (703) 948–4955. Dates to 1926. Sells groceries, general merchandise, and deli sandwiches. Located at intersection of routes 230 and 662.

The Mayberry Trading Post in Virginia

West Virginia

Cass Country Store, Cass, WV 24927; (304) 456–4491. Established in 1902. Sells gifts and souvenirs; it is said this was once the largest company store in America—it served a logging community during the early 1900s. Located in Cass, near the Cass Scenic Railroad depot.

Wyoming

Fort Laramie Sutler's Store (part of Fort Laramie National Historic Site), Fort Laramie, WY 82212; (307) 837–2221. Dates to 1849—a fur trading post was established here as early as 1834. Store serves as a museum. Located off U.S. 26 at Laramie National Historical Site.

Country stores appeal to all the senses, even to the musical sense of these mountain pickers at the Mayberry Trading Post near the Blue Ridge Parkway in Virginia.